T0131796

PROVING HEAVEN 2.0

Fix and Upgrade Broken Faith Through a Deep Understanding of the Real Heaven!

Raymond Kresha, MEd, LPC

BALBOA.
PRESS
A DIVISION OF HAY HOUSE

Balboa Press books may be ordered through booksellers or by contacting:

Balboa Press
A Division of Hay House
1663 Liberty Drive
Bloomington, IN 47403
www.balboapress.com
1 (877) 407-4847

Print information available on the last page.

ISBN: 978-1-5043-8340-0 (sc)
ISBN: 978-1-5043-8341-7 (hc)
ISBN: 978-1-5043-8383-7 (e)

Library of Congress Control Number: 2017910124

Balboa Press rev. date: 07/11/2017

ACKNOWLEDGEMENTS

Special thanks to Gloria Thomas for her editing and input into making this book as good as it can be.

Thanks to E. Russell Lambert for his comments and insights on atheism, as it helped inform the shape this text has taken. Thanks to Robert Kolar and Lilita Olano for comments and advice regarding content and presentation.

Thanks to the many writers and authors who have come before, without which this text would be impossible. These include Jane Roberts, Gary Renard, Kenneth Wapnick, and Helen Schucman and Bill Thetford, scribes of A Course in Miracles.

Thanks and appreciation for the guidance and instruction from the Holy Spirit through my lifetime, answering questions and showing me the way back home!

Thanks to Wikipedia for being there for fact-checking and getting references correct. They definitely deserve appreciation for making information and history available to the masses without long treks to specialized libraries and other repositories of knowledge.

CONTENTS

PART 5   HEAVENLY FAQ'S

INTRODUCTION

Have you ever felt like things in Life aren't right? You work hard at life and try to get as close to perfect as possible, yet things often fall apart? Do bad things happen to good people, no matter how hard you try? It seems that too often good things happen to people acting badly. Liars manipulate things to get their own way, promising a better life, yet never delivering. It seems like life is insane.

We want a utopia, a place where everything is perfect and we work toward it. We believe if we work hard enough, do the right things and cajole others long enough, we can make the world a better, maybe perfect, place. We try and try, but the Good Life seems to elude us. A lot of people just don't "get" it and ruin it for everybody else. For some, social and environmental consciousness, eating vegan, loving all living things isn't as popular as it should. For others, following their inner guidance and trying new things without interference from others is their goal. Some want a god-like government to enforce utopian ideas; others idea of utopia is to be left alone to live their lives in peace and harmony, as long as they don't interfere with the rights of anybody else. People seldom agree for long. Something isn't right.

But what to do?

We see ourselves as unique and wonderful individuals. We revel in this distinctiveness that sets us apart from all others. We feel separate, yet acknowledge a bond we would like to strengthen, at least with some people. How can we make a better world when so many are obnoxious and despicable and don't want to change? How is utopia possible with so many different kinds of people?

People have found that if they answer these questions certain ways, they can manipulate others for their own benefit. Churches and governments have a good purpose, but are often dominated by individuals who use the emotional and physical power they wield to get their own needs and wants met as well. Too often Truth and the wants and needs of the many are subservient to those of the few. Spirituality gets lost. Some people actually get hurt.

The focus on our individuality and separateness is the de facto point of view for human life. It is axiomatic that heaven must be physical because we are physical, we are our bodies. We believe there can be no heaven without bodies because we wouldn't be us without them. That is why we believe in and search for a physical Heaven for our physical body: we call it Heaven 1.0. It has yet to be found.

Perhaps it is time to look at Heaven differently and see the other vision of Heaven, referred to here as 2.0. It is a more complete, understandable vision of what Heaven is really all about. This upgrade in understanding looks past the body to lose what is illusion and no longer helps. It provides a greater comprehension of the eternal Reality.

Oneness, the Big Bang, good and evil, love and hate, Heaven and Hell, birth and death all can be understood in a way that makes sense. In a genuine way, we all must come to terms with this enigma, for our personal future depends upon it. Many have likened life to a merry-go-round or the wheel of life; it goes around and round... until we decide to get off. Only you can decide if life as you know it is an endless waste of time. If so, you can move on to more and better.

The bottom line is that the Utopia many seek to create on Earth already exists and it always has. Most of us have a deep inner feeling that there is more, that things can be better, despite appearances to the contrary. Building a permanent heaven in our physical world is both impossible and unnecessary. Heaven 2.0 is perfect Oneness and has always been. Have we merely forgotten it?

Many of us dimly remember a different way, an infinitely more pleasurable way of life. We believe we are a part of something much greater, much more powerful and fulfilling. The physical life we live on Earth is nothing compared to the eye-opening remembrance or enlightenment beyond the veil we have placed over our inner sight.

Many have tried to describe Heaven 2.0 and words often fail. Decades have gone into the writing of this description and it isn't so much the description of Heaven that is the main issue, but more the many reasons that get in the way of remembering Heaven. It was *A Course in Miracles* that outlined the many blocks that we have put in place to keep things just the way they are, yet left open the way to enlightenment. When we remember who we really are, we can remove those blocks. From the eternal viewpoint of Heaven, it has already happened: we all remembered and re-entered the Light. No one was forced. Our free will dictates it must be our choice.

For this reason, the task of Proving Heaven must look at why so many value individuality, uniqueness and specialness more than a Oneness that must include all the people we hate in life. Why do we condemn some of our siblings, also created from our same Source? The task of building a Heaven on Earth only for those who are good enough also seems to mean building a Hell somewhere else to send those who aren't good enough or won't go along.

Spiritual masters often talk of finding a way past these dilemmas, by eliminating desire and practicing forgiveness. The task first must be to want Heaven more than we want life on Earth. We have to decide which is more important. Those who have remembered Oneness have let the light of Truth shine into their lives and left the prison we have fashioned for ourselves. Once we remember there is no locked door, it's only a matter of removing the lies we have told ourselves and piled in front of that open door.

Words have twisted up our understanding of Life and Love yet perhaps words can be used to untangle this multi-faceted mess. It is important to get a personal understanding of our Source so that words are no longer necessary. No more bibles or handbooks. Once you remember, you cannot forget. After all, the books are here only to help us get to remembrance, to illumination. After we get to the top of the mountain of illusions we have created, the view is always the same: Love.

This book should never be taken to denigrate any church or religion. They are doing the best they can with what they've got. Some want to go beyond calcified dogma and move on into direct Unity. Call it meditation, prayer, or Union, we all seek to return to Oneness by any means available to us. This text is just one way to help you get back on the path.

If Oneness, the essence of Heaven 2.0, makes sense to you, then perhaps this little quotation will make sense:

> To be one is to be of one mind or will. When the will of [humanity] and [our Source] are one, then perfect accord is Heaven. —*A Course in Miracles* (ACIM)

SECTION ONE
THE LANDSCAPE

CHAPTER 1
READ THIS FIRST

If you haven't read the "Introduction," please do so; it will help you understand how and why this book is put together the way it is. It is not like any other. It is more about remembering the pathway to Truth and removing the rubble in our way.

There are books that set out to prove the existence of Heaven through the experience of others. This is wonderful, since if one person can experience Heaven, we all can. This text is very different in that it sets out to prove the existence of Heaven because it must be, because it has always existed. However, proof and heaven are two of the most misunderstood words in any language. It has been necessary, to refine their definitions to even have a chance. These definitions aren't new, merely forgotten by many.

It has even been necessary to invent the structure of this book, as it doesn't fit well into existing genres. It's a problem of expectations. Here we are building an argument and it would be helpful to read it and consider it, in order. This will help you gain a stronger understanding of Heaven 2.0. It is most effective if you read all parts of the argument, which tends to build sequentially; it isn't just a collection of facts.

It is necessary to find the flaws in our usual assumptions and definitions and look at the evidence around us with new eyes, else we continue to miss the mark. The most important way to approach this subject is that you must be open to seeing both proof and Heaven differently.

Proof is more than what a mathematician or scientist may require. In a way, it is like a jury. Proof is what the members accept as verification and fits in with the facts and their experience. Many people believe in Heaven, but don't remember why and would be hard put to explain it logically. We set out to do this.

If one is to consider understanding Heaven, it is helpful to start with core assumptions and consider your beliefs as to who we are, how we got here, where we are going and what the "end" will look like. Some assumptions are wrong. It is why we look to atheists to point out the problems of Heaven 1.0. Heaven 1.0 doesn't work for many people, precipitating the need for an upgrade.

There are many spiritual belief systems; Wikipedia mentions 4,200 different religions. Christianity is reputed to have over 33,000 denominations. They are wonderful, are "good enough" and work great—until they don't. This book is for those for whom traditional ideas are inadequate, though not necessarily wrong. This book provides a deeper explanation and corrects minor misunderstandings based on the belief that we are a physical body. If you need more, once you realize you are already in Heaven, answers will flow to you from Heaven regarding life's dilemmas, without need of somebody to tell you.

Looking at the problems atheists have with modern religious ideas really is a good place to start, since they are willing to point out areas of inadequacy. It is very useful to review their thoughts, since if they can be answered, it might be beneficial for all concerned. All believers want a deeper understanding and a stronger belief. Those who are stuck and no longer believe, might want to figure out what is holding them back. We must look at what the atheists are saying, not in anger, but in gratitude because they point out blind spots in what is being taught by many of today's teachers. This book is an encouragement for those who are seeking on their own, choosing not to wait until traditional command and control sources change what they teach.

The great religious teachers lived hundreds of years ago and yet, despite the passage of so much time, mankind does not seem to have made a lot of progress. Could it be that we have built barriers to keep our lives pretty much as they are, spiritually? There have been wars, genocides, slavery, and many forms of anger and trauma throughout history and it appears they are still happening today. It is for this reason that these blocks must be looked at because if we do not become aware of them, we will continue to do what we have always done; as the saying goes, the more things change: the more they stay the same. Truth often becomes clichéd because it is the Truth.

We really have to talk about why people say they want to go to Heaven, but would not give up their body to do so. What is going on? Very few people would go to Heaven TODAY, if given the choice to continue living on earth or die to go to Heaven. Maybe we aren't too sure that Heaven exists or we don't understand what it is really like. Maybe we just like it here.

[An aside: most suicides do so to get away from a painful situation or to punish someone else, not to go directly to Heaven. However, some suicide bombers seem to reason this way: do the will of Allah and go to heaven immediately.]

If you think about it, we really do value our bodies and are really "attached" to them, literally and figuratively. We are highly focused on the five senses in the here-and-now. Even if we hate our bodies and what is happening to them, we remain steadfast in thinking only about its welfare.

Despite the fact that our lifetime is limited and has a beginning and an end, it is the only life we think we know. The fact that we must use words to communicate is a barrier to people understanding each other. Unfortunately, words mean different things to different people, especially if it is a different sub-culture or language. The temporary nature of our lifetime as an individual and the need to use indirect symbols to communicate (words) constitute barriers to meaningful discussions about Heaven. For now, that seems to be all we have. Those who can communicate directly (i.e. psychics or empaths) are often discounted.

It is also important to note that this book uses the word "Heaven" and seldom the word "God" because of the enormous baggage that the word "God" carries in people's minds. It is also important to realize that God is not a person in the same sense that we are a separate person. On the other hand, for those who seek a "personal relationship" with God, you cannot get more personal than Oneness. Ultimately there is only one "Person." Oneness transfigures ideas of individuality and specialness as we remember our native Nondual state of Reality. We will also use synonyms for Heaven 2.0 to include Oneness, All-That-Is, Life, Truth, all capitalized. Oneness has many names: see chapter 4.

Our job in life is the undoing of ideas of separateness and remembering that we are Love incarnate and an inseparable part of All-That-Is eternally. All-That-Is is just a name for looking at all that exists, in any way or fashion. There are many ways to accomplish this release of our sense of individuality, but expressing Love for our neighbors and forgiving them when needed is often a big part of it. Once we find out what it feels like to be really one with others, aloneness loses all attractiveness.

This is why Parts One and Two are written the way they are. If you don't know all the obstacles that must be dealt with, it will be difficult to make progress. In other words, one must really want to move past the evidence of the senses, words, definitions, and other evidence against Heaven. Miss that and you miss the main point of this text.

Part Three starts with a strong reasoned argument that if Heaven 2.0 is All-That-Is, then It is all-powerful, all-knowing, all-loving, eternal, everywhere-present and more. Properly understood, It cannot be otherwise. This view of Heaven is ancient, yet new age. It has been known throughout history. We examine many different kinds of evidence, including channeling and near-death experiences. It is important to talk about the amazing innate abilities we have, things such as free will, the ability to create, to believe, to inspire and to image.

Section Four looks at the value of faith and trust in our search for Heaven 2.0. Building a belief system you can believe in and one that is strong enough to support your faith is the primary goal of this volume. It is a guide to peeling away the false beliefs that get in the way and adding new ideas that strengthen our resolve. Recognizing what is false is the key. The use of parables, stories, and myths are often helpful in our remembering that we are already in Heaven. There is nowhere else.

It is helpful to note that when you find a pathway that works for you, stay on it. Try not to wander off in search of "something better." All pathways eventually lead to Truth and all good paths require study and learning a mental discipline. This takes time, effort and commitment. Regularly changing paths sets one back because you have to start all over again with a new discipline and shows lack of effort and commitment. Don't fall asleep again and forget.

The closer one comes to the end goal of remembering Oneness, the more important it becomes to see Oneness in all we meet, even politicians we don't like. One guide to evaluate a path is how important an all-encompassing Love is on that path. It is said the only real answer to every question is Love. Once you understand why that is so, you will have no problem restructuring your life to make that your experience as well. If the path helps you do this, all is well.

The final section, Part Five, the FAQ's, is presented with a sense of humor and a hint as to what it looks like when we "approach" Heaven 2.0. It might be different than you expect. Heaven 2.0 is an upgrade from the first version of Heaven, which is very much like our physical planet Earth, where we get to keep our bodies and live in them forever. Creating Heaven on Earth is literally Heaven 1.0. It sounds attractive because it maintains separate identities. Waking up is much easier than creating a Utopian illusion of togetherness. What we have forgotten is how much fun Heaven 2.0 is and much, much more. The FAQ's point out some of the chaff or false ideas surrounding our thoughts about Heaven 2.0.

It is important to overcome the fear of Heaven and the accompanying guilt, as did the young man in the parable of the Prodigal Son. It is worth it for Heaven 2.0 is really All-Loving. Imagine a party with everyone you have ever loved and the ones you thought you hated, you love even more! The idea that we are separate from Heaven is insidious and a part of many theologies. With it comes error thinking that leads to exactly what we have now: chaos and insanity mixed in with the love and caring.

There is a much better way of looking at Life.

CHAPTER 2
THANK GOD FOR ATHEISTS

There are many people who don't believe in Heaven, especially the 1.0 version. We should be grateful to atheists and agnostics for highlighting the areas of faith that don't make sense and work toward a) finding the truth and b) clarifying inconsistencies.

It's very useful to look at atheists' arguments since their reasoning tends to illuminate the entire process of proving Heaven. As many have noted, our best efforts should be geared toward finding what is false in life more than trying to determine what is true. Everything appears to be true when it's seen or heard, but not everything is as it appears.

A case in point: while "seeing may be believing," it's easy to prove that not everything we see is true. Optical illusions, magic tricks, and edited videos can present information to us that is more propaganda than documentary. Our atheist friends are a big help in finding beliefs that make no sense. As many sages have noted, we all have some of the truth, but none of us has all of it; therefore, it's beneficial to listen to those who ask us to think twice about our concepts about God and Heaven. Many religious books are internally contradictory, and we should be grateful for those who point out these issues, even if they are beloved beliefs that have stood for a really long time. Blind faith is helpful at first, but it is a consistent informed faith that becomes wisdom.

Here are the four biggest and most frequently mentioned areas of conflict between believers and atheists regarding Heaven 1.0:

1. There is little scientific evidence of God.
2. There are inconsistent "revelations" among religions.
3. Religion doesn't adequately address the problem of evil.
4. Some believers make nonsensical arguments in favor of God's existence.

A note: the word "God" and male pronouns are used in this chapter because they are the common and expected nomenclature in discussions of Heaven 1.0. Gender has no place in Heaven 2.0 and "It" will be used to highlight the non-gender aspect of nondual Oneness.

Scientific Evidence for a Physical, Personal God Is Missing

Evidence from the five senses proving the existence of a physical, personal God is hard to come by. What is evidence for a believer is dismissed and reinterpreted by a skeptic. The problem is that people expect a physical heaven, but none can be found. Let's look closer.

Despite the lack of evidence, the belief in a personal very physical God is common and perhaps pervasive in most religions. From the 72 virgins an Islamic martyr might expect to sleep with to Saint Paul's ideas about the afterlife and the final judgment, one can say the importance of a physical body is paramount to many religious belief systems. Some think Heaven is a place and God is a "person" who lives there. Many people's ideas about Heaven are merely an expansion of physical life, but "with benefits."

It should be mentioned here that many Islamic scholars say there is no promise of virgins for martyrs in the Quran. They say it stems from a poor translation of one section, 78:29–34. Accepted translations vary from "companions of equal age" to "young full-breasted maidens of equal age." There is no number of companions mentioned in the text. (justislam. co.uk)

Upon examination, most religions appear to assume that Heaven is a kind of quasi-physical place, one where our physical bodies would be happy, perhaps in a "perfected" state of some type. It's entirely understandable how one might come to believe this after reading the scriptures. Either our bodies in Heaven are physical in the same sense as they are here, or they aren't. It's that simple. The problem comes in when people try to combine incompatible beliefs.

However, many theologians' explanations are very clear. The Catholic website, catholic.com, says this about the resurrection of the body after death, even if it's after many centuries:

> The Bible tells us that when Jesus returns to earth, he will physically raise all those who have died, giving them back the bodies they lost at death. These will be the same bodies people

had in earthly life —but our resurrected bodies will not die, and, for the righteous, they will be transformed into a glorified state, freed from suffering and pain, and enabled to do many of the amazing things Jesus could do with his glorified body (1 Cor. 15:35—44, 1 John 3:2).

The resurrection of the body is an essential Christian doctrine, as the apostle Paul declares: "If the dead are not raised, then Christ has not been raised. If Christ has not been raised, your faith is futile and you are still in your sins. Then those also who have fallen asleep in Christ have perished" (1 Cor. 15:13—18).

It couldn't be clearer.

Most uneducated people throughout history have thought of themselves as essentially physical, and most religious teaching has capitalized on that to start people on the road to faith, hope, and charity. A physical heaven is something people could relate to. Religions talk about Heaven as an eternal place of happiness and reward for good behavior. Thousands of years ago, politicians realized that this idea could also be used as a tool to coerce people into doing what they wanted them to do in this life. They promised a reward after death, and rewards in a physical Heaven are more potent motivators than abstract rewards in a spiritual place.

Catholic Church history describes how, in 325 CE, at the first Council of Nicaea, a Creed or statement of beliefs was voted on, saying Jesus is the only Son of God, born of the Virgin Mary, and sits at the right hand of God. This Creed requires Christians to see the Heaven where God is as a quasi-physical place, not unlike Earth. Just where it's located wasn't specified, but biblical writers seemed to indicate that it's up in the sky. The Bible describes Jesus floating up into heaven (the Ascension), meaning into the sky above (similar to ascents by the ancient Jewish prophets Enoch and Elijah):

> ...he was taken up into a cloud while they were watching, and they could no longer see him. As they strained to see him rising into heaven, two white-robed men suddenly stood among them. "Men of Galilee," they said, "why are you standing here staring into heaven? Jesus has been taken from you into heaven, but someday he will return from heaven in the same way you saw him go!" (Acts 1:9––11, New Living Translation)

This conception of Heaven is emphasized in the Gospel of John, who quotes Jesus as saying:

> When everything is ready, I will come and get you, so that you will always be with me where I am. (John 14:3, New Living Translation)

This verse isn't specific as to what form this "place" might take, but most people have assumed that they would be taken physically and alive. Many believe that this promises a physical "rapture," an instant removal from the physical world into a physical heaven.

Then there is the Book of Revelation. Many get their ideas about Heaven from Saint John, who wrote while in a cave near present-day Turkey, in exile, on the island of Patmos.

> I heard a loud shout from the throne, saying, "Look, God's home is now among his people! He will live with them, and they will be his people. God himself will be with them. He will wipe every tear from their eyes, and there will be no more death or sorrow or crying or pain. All these things are gone forever." And the one sitting on the throne said, "Look, I am making everything new!" (Revelation 21:3—5, New Living Translation)

This makes God like a man, able to live with them and wipe their tears away. He has a throne just like earthly kings and emperors. Further in that same chapter, St. John also describes the dwelling of God as a city and calls it the "new Jerusalem." This new description is fantastic, specific, and physical:

> The angel who talked to me held in his hand a gold measuring stick to measure the city, its gates, and its wall. When he measured it, he found it was a square, as wide as it was long. In fact, its length and width and height were

each 1,400 miles. Then he measured the walls and found them to be 216 feet thick (according to the human standard used by the angel). The wall was made of jasper, and the city was pure gold, as clear as glass. The wall of the city was built on foundation stones inlaid with twelve precious stones: the first was jasper, the second sapphire, the third agate, the fourth emerald, the fifth onyx, the sixth carnelian, the seventh chrysolite, the eighth beryl, the ninth topaz, the tenth chrysoprase, the eleventh jacinth, the twelfth amethyst. (Revelation 21:15–21, Berean Study Bible)

St. John describes Heaven as a huge *cube*, not unlike the Borg Collective in Star Trek! This is the source of common references to Heaven 1.0 as the place of the "pearly gates" and having "streets of gold." Those who take this description of heaven literally believe that Heaven is 1,400 miles wide, deep and high. By the way, the moon is 2,160 miles wide. If Heaven were truly a physical place, at roughly two-thirds the size of the moon, it would be visible to the Hubble Space Telescope, which can see billions of light-years into space. So say many atheists and others.

With many scientists exploring space in recent decades, both in space vehicles and through the Hubble Telescope, it can be reasonably demonstrated that a square object that size can't be found. This does lend credence to the argument that Heaven isn't a physical place. If heaven is not physical then one wouldn't need a physical body after death, glorified or otherwise. It's no wonder that people get confused on this critical point and come to all sorts of conclusions that often conflict with the core message of the religion.

Statues and drawings of God have been prevalent in most religions and churches throughout history though Islam permits no images of Mohammad or Allah. Statues in India, drawings in the caves of prehistoric people, and artifacts in the pyramids in Egypt are just a few examples. They apparently were popular with uneducated, illiterate people, who could relate to a Deity that was very much like their parents. The idea of God being a super-person with a physical body and a home (Heaven) was comforting and made Him approachable. However, since people couldn't fly, Heaven in the sky was also a very convenient place for the priestly class to put God since no one could go there and check on His existence. The idea of God being both physical and personal is also embedded deeply in many Christians' thinking, often as the result of relentless religious teachings that the Deity is a person not unlike themselves.

For these reasons, most atheists have no patience with the concept of a physical God. With the advent of the printing press and mass distribution of books, it could be pointed out that Jesus himself didn't talk about heaven as physical. It's difficult to say just how it started, but it's hard to deny that the concept of a physical heaven plays into the hands of church leaders who found it useful in getting church members to financially support the church and its physical needs. This probably escalated when the church became closely associated with kings, queens, and emperors, all demanding money on behalf of God. Many leaders let people think they themselves were God incarnate or that they ruled by divine right. Atheists and many others have a hard time accepting spiritual ideas from those who are actively controlling believers in ways that get their own physical wants and needs met first, living in the lap of luxury.

For a long time, thinking people have rejected the idea of a physical God or Heaven due to a lack of concrete evidence. It's logical, then, to assume the worst: if there is no evidence, there is no God and no Heaven. It's not an argument that satisfies, yet it's honest. That's why we should be grateful to atheists for highlighting this problem.

Inconsistent Religious Revelations

All religions believe that God revealed Himself to mankind through specific teachers, many of whom wrote down what was revealed about Heaven to them. One of the biggest problems with Heaven 1.0 is that there aren't very many written descriptions of Heaven, and those that do exist conflict with each other. There are many thousands of religious groups claiming to have the true theology of God.

If you would like to see how inconsistent things have become, look at Wikipedia, which says there are about 4,200 religions in the world. They do not all agree. If you are Christian, the "List of Christian Denominations" shows over 33,000+ denominations. The tantalizing point is, if God physically exists as a separate person and wants people to behave a certain way, would He not make it clear to all His children throughout history just exactly what He expects? Would it not be the same behaviors if the requirements were from the same source? The extreme numbers and variations are evidence of there *not* being one God and of people just making it up as they go along, for their own purposes.

The very fact that there are so many people telling other people what to believe, combined with the huge variation in what those beliefs are, is enough to make any thinking person stop and consider.

One of the most insidious degradations of spiritual principles is what is called "moral relativism," the idea that moral judgments are only held to be true relative to some particular viewpoint and that there is no viewpoint that is better than any other. It is the epitome of inconsistent revelations: truth is relative and so are moral judgments. There is no one god, one religion, or single standard upon which to judge life.

An example is whether all lies are bad. Are "white lies" OK because someone's feelings are spared? A big one is whether all killing of another is bad or not. Is killing somebody OK when defending one's self, property, or loved ones? In fact, killing enemies is often celebrated. Some think lying and killing are morally bad only relative to why you did it. Some religious people can justify nearly any activity, weakening teachings about what is True and what is not. Hate and fear can be used to justify nearly any immoral act.

Religion and Evil

The main issue for many nonbelievers is that religion doesn't adequately address the problem of evil. If God created everything, why did He create evil or even the capacity for evil? It's a very good question, one most churches tend to avoid. "It's a mystery" isn't good enough, especially for atheists or agnostics.

Evil is described as something that is profoundly immoral that comes about when people intentionally cause harm to others. Often evil seems to have "a mind of its own," causing many to think of it as a force or a person. Note the word "evil" in "devil." People are sometimes called devils for what they have done. Humans have a great capacity to think of anything the way they want to, and humans often personify inanimate objects. Just because we can give a car or an animal a name and assign human traits to it doesn't make it a person. In the same sense, just because someone does something evil doesn't make them the devil incarnate. There is no one person whom everyone would say is "the devil."

Atheists often point to the evil in the world as evidence that there is either no God or one they cannot believe in. If there is a God, then God is Itself evil, having created wickedness. At best, the world is an insane place, a mixture of beauty and wonder mixed in with death, destruction, trauma, and hatred. If one believes in a God who is good, yet is seemingly capable of creating or allowing evil, atheists feel justified in deciding not to believe in such a demented conflicted God.

How does a believer reconcile belief in a God who is good and loving yet allows tremendous amounts of suffering, sickness, trauma, and other arguably tragic events in the world? Wouldn't a good God who knows everything do something about it or prevent it? If God created everything, why would He create even the possibility of evil and then punish those who are tripped up by that evil through no fault of their own? If there is a fault, that defect was created by God because the fault lies with the Creator. Such a God would be evil by just about any standard. Claims of inscrutability or that "God's ways are not our ways" just won't cut it for most thinking people. Very few people are drawn to a God who is incompetent, insane, or evil.

Beyond who created evil, would a loving God, who knows everything, allow evil to stand unabated? No loving human parent would fail to do anything they could to protect their own offspring. How, then, can an imperfect loving parent do a better job of loving than our supposedly perfect loving God? It's very easy to point out ways in which God is clearly not always a loving creator, at least in the theologies of most Western religions. It's a potent argument.

In fact, far from being a force for peace, God and religions seem to be the cause of many wars and much intolerance. Here is a brief excerpt from an article by Louise Ridley, a writer at the Huffington Post's UK website, quoting Richard Dawkins on the subject:

It is the most common comeback from atheists to people of faith: religion is the main cause of wars. Without faith, many say, there would have been no 9/11 attacks, no Israeli-Palestinian conflict, no troubles in Northern Ireland, no violent disputes over words in holy texts—even no Islamic State.

Richard Dawkins, Britain's best-known atheist, has argued that religion has been the main cause of violence and war throughout history. He wrote in his 2013 autobiography that "religion is the principal label, and the most dangerous one, by which a "they," as opposed to a "we," can be identified."

Dawkins has said that if religion were somehow abolished, there would be "a much better chance of no more war." There would also be "less hatred, because a lot of the hatred in the world is sectarian hatred," according to Dawkins. "For example, in Northern Ireland, India, and Pakistan," he told the website belief.net.

Dawkins, a former professor at Oxford, is the author of *The God Delusion*.

War isn't the only kind of evil one can find. Often, it's found on an individual, personal level. If one sees others as different from oneself, they can be seen as a threat. It's often said that fear is the opposite of love. If we don't know someone or love them, then there is always a bit of fear. Beyond that, how does it happen that people we love or who love us can turn on us and do evil things to us? It seems that things are very unstable in our personal lives and evil seems to live inside each of us, given the amount of harm we have caused ourselves and others. Let's not quibble about the word "evil," for it's amazing how fast a mild irritation can become a violent tragedy for some of us. This indicates that there is something wrong with human beings as created by God.

Let's not forget that we often project our fears onto others, making them the enemy, precipitating violence and evil.

Atheists point out that evil seems to win a great deal of the time, often going unpunished, and good people often are unrewarded for virtuous and righteous behavior. Apologists often defend God by saying that humans were created with free will. However, atheists counter with the argument, "Why give a creation something if you hope they never use it for evil? If a father gives his eight-year-old child a loaded gun, does he really expect him never to try to shoot it? Why give it to him in the first place?"

One acknowledgment of a flawed creation is the Christian doctrine of "original sin," originating from the "fall of man." This is the biblical story of the tree in the Garden of Eden. Why would God feed Adam and Eve with the fruit of many trees and other plants in the Garden, yet put one there they must not eat from? Tempting vulnerable people is a special kind of evil, even in this world. The lesson is that God is not to be trusted. Did not God also create the snake to make sure it happened? If God is good, why create a trap <u>and</u> a tempter to push Adam and Eve into it? God put the means and the temptation in place for the fall of humankind. Why, if it wasn't meant to happen? If you can't trust God, who can you trust?

And didn't Adam's son Cain kill his brother Abel? This story of love turning to hate is found in the Christian Bible, the Jewish Torah, and the Muslim Quran. Somehow, just explaining that human beings have free will doesn't let the Creator off the hook, a God who claims to be perfect Love and Peace, yet He created a "son" destined to fall and become evil.

There are many kinds of harm that can befall humans and other life in this physical world, and it seems to be built-in. One can see how an atheist might doubt a Being that would create a world with death, scarcity, sickness, and insanity in it. These are valid reasons to doubt traditional versions of a personal God and Heaven 1.0.

The atheists are right: traditional answers don't satisfy, and the argument over evil continues unabated on the physical Earth. There must be more to the story.

Nonsensical Philosophical Arguments

Many atheists, scientists included, are wonderful, creative, caring people. Many are very intelligent and active in fields that require proof of one kind or another. One problem they have in believing in God is that, for them, if something can't be proven to exist, then perhaps it doesn't. Others say there is room for doubt since God can't be proven *not* to exist except by viewing life as purely physical. Often the problem is in the way God is defined: many people's vision of an anthropomorphic super-man God is not likely to exist anywhere except in their imaginations. To many religions, God is physical in some respect.

In general, a physical heaven can't be proven not to exist. It's kind of like being a devil's advocate: if one can prove that Heaven can't exist, the argument is over. If you can't prove it doesn't exist, believers reason, this is evidence that it might exist. One potential reason for our failure to prove that Heaven doesn't exist is, of course, that it does. It's tough to find agreement in any case, and words are often a roadblock to precise, meaningful communication.

For those who are interested, this idea of proving negatives is illustrated by "Russell's teapot." It's a perfect example of showing the futility of trying to prove something by pointing out that the proof lies somewhere that isn't accessible. Bertrand Russell, a well-known philosopher and atheist in the mid-1900s, said that if he asserted that there is a small china teapot orbiting the sun in an elliptical orbit, it would be impossible to prove him wrong. The teapot would be too small to be seen by even the most powerful telescopes or devices in existence, he stated. Russell argued that it wouldn't be reasonable to believe in the existence of the teapot merely because one couldn't disprove its existence. He was critical of believers who vilified him for his doubts about the existence of God or Heaven, saying it's nonsense for the believers to insist that It exists merely because they believe it.

Many people try to prove their ideas simply by noting that they are written in ancient texts; but just because it's written, Russell argued, doesn't prove the texts are correct. Russell contended that people who believe in God have the burden of proof for their belief, not the one who doesn't believe. In other words, proof must come from the believer before that believer insists that someone else believe the same way that they do.

It's OK if people believe different things about God. It's not OK for people to impose their beliefs on others and still insist that it's the loving thing to do. There are few words or solid definitions of God or Heaven that can be accepted by all people and religions.

Thankfully, agnostics and other doubters help keep us honest and seeking better answers instead of merely accepting answers that were more appropriate to those who couldn't read for themselves and had to rely on others. Thank God for atheists—they keep us honest on our journey to understand ourselves, our world, and how it all came to be.

SECTION TWO
BARRIERS TO PROOF

CHAPTER 3
WHY WE DON'T WANT HEAVEN

Home Is Where Our Heart Is

We have looked at why atheists don't believe in Heaven 1.0. Theirs is a thoughtful, principled judgment on the existence of something that they can't physically perceive. To summarize, there is no science and no agreement on what Heaven is or looks like. Evil continues to be a major problem and some people just get silly and irrational in their arguments for Heaven.

Even among religious people there are some fairly deep negative feelings about Heaven, given the heavy religious drumbeat counseling people to avoid "sin" and to accept certain beliefs or face the fires of Hell. Most people have a hard time living up to the ten commandments and other dictums, such as "love your neighbor" when he or she has done something wrong. Many talk about forgiving others for their sins, yet forgiveness is hard because it appears that you are rewarding people for their misbehaviors or letting them off the hook when they should be punished. Many believe justice demands retribution or punishment.

When we think about ourselves, most of us recognize that we have made mistakes. Since the bar that guarantees entry into Heaven is pretty high, many doubt they have been good enough to make it. Trouble is, there is no reliable score-keeping while we are alive. We have to wait until *after* we die to find out what happens. What if it's rigged against us? For many, it's either Heaven or Hell. For some, there is an in-between place, but there is a lot of disagreement on that. If we haven't been perfect and others tell us we are sinners, and our parents' voices in our head tell us we are no good, then it's reasonable to entertain the idea that we might not make it to Heaven.

If Heaven is everywhere, we have forgotten it completely. We have to do our best. Some people don't believe in Heaven at all, and they seem to be happy enough. Many others may say they believe in Heaven, but they really don't want to go there anytime soon. Living our life with our loved ones seems to be a much more attractive here-and-now option, while eternal unlimited happiness is a big unknown and not guaranteed.

In any case, our bodies and our planet appear to be our home. Heaven is far away; our loved ones are close by. Why would we want to go anywhere else? There are many different ideas on just what Heaven is and what one must do to get there. So, it might be better to just spend our time enjoying our friends and family. As the saying goes, "Heaven can wait."

Many religious people say we were created in the image and likeness of God. Are they right? We sometimes see beauty in other people, art, animals, and the natural landscape. There is a beauty in the workings of the seasons, the solar system, and even the natural order of life and death. Earth is beautiful seen from space. Photos taken by the Hubble Telescope of distant galaxies contrast with the microscopic order of our bodies and the subatomic world. PBS's series *Nova* and other programs often showcase the natural beauty of the world in a way that is hard to deny.

Is evil in the world part of God too, of whom we are a mirror image? Despite the beauty that exists in the world, the definition of Hell is "anywhere where Heaven is not." Many would describe their earthly lives as Hell. While some people experience idyllic lives, others find the exact opposite, that is, hatred, war, sickness, scarcity, jealousy, slavery, torture, and just about anything else a person might be able to imagine. Our world is of a split mind, part wonderful, part hellish, depending on when and where somebody is looking.

There are at least two key ideas here. One is that evidence of Heaven isn't easily found in the physical world, leading many to not believe in Heaven 1.0 at all and to believe that this is the only world that exists. Some scientists consider all things mental to be illusions and epiphenomenal, a byproduct of the body. The second idea is that since almost none of us wish to die right *now,* even if we are guaranteed to go straight to Heaven, we really don't want to go to Heaven. Not right now. With no solid guarantees and no visible guarantor, there are few volunteers. Those who commit suicide are making a bet that the next world is better than this one or don't even care if there is another one, judging that no world is better than the one causing the pain they are feeling.

Our death is inevitable; it's something we can be sure of. How or if we think about it is our choice. Many of us choose to focus on our bodies and the world we live in and not think about the future unless we are forced to, either with a personal close call or the loss of a loved one. At times like that, it's obvious that life is temporary and the Earth isn't our permanent home.

Even though we know this, there seems to be something in us that prefers the physical world we live in and that causes us to resist thinking about what comes next. Even threats of eternal damnation aren't enough to move many people, especially if they don't believe in it. People have the capacity to act first and think later, before the inevitable consequences of their actions are realized. Anger and a fight can result in prison. Drinking and driving can result in motor vehicle homicide. Things just seem to happen.

What's going on?

When we consider where our real home might be, here on Earth or somewhere else, we would really rather not have the conversation. Even those who want to go to Heaven find problems that block their progress, despite their desire to move forward. The seminal spiritual book *A Course in Miracles* (*ACIM*), scribed by Dr. Helen Schucman, discusses what are called "blocks to the remembrance of Heaven." This chapter in this book had its origins in *ACIM*'s brief discussion of why people really don't want to go to Heaven. Most us appear to want to remain spiritually asleep in the physical world; few want to "wake up and go home," Heaven 2.0. This is changing as people get tired of the status quo.

This chapter expands significantly on why people don't want to immediately go to an eternally loving and peaceful place. The psychological and emotional barriers that we have put into place must be examined and overcome if we are to make serious progress toward upgrading our ideas on Heaven. Whether one believes in the Rapture, enlightenment, or just living the law of love, one must recognize and resolve this hindering issue.

Block 1:
Wanting to Get Rid of Heaven

Perhaps Genesis got some of it right: we are here in physical form on Earth because of choices made in Paradise. This metaphorical story tells how humans were created and why they are the way they are. It was written by human beings for others here on Earth. The Creator is painted as responsible for duality, i.e. Eve. God knows that duality is problematic and tried to dissuade the first couple from experimenting with full-blown separateness from Heaven. They chose to do so, "eating the apple" of life and death and good and evil. True separation is not possible, so they wound up with a dream, a mirror of Heaven, to see what it would be like. Adam fell asleep, no longer aware of the Oneness of Paradise. The bible never talks about him waking up.

The choice had consequences. We descendants of Adam and Eve are living and exploring that choice right now. We decided once that we didn't want the real Heaven. We later discovered that our self-made heaven wasn't perfect, so we have been busy ever since trying to create heaven on Earth and completely eradicate all traces of the real Heaven. This apparently went from just experiencing separation to a flat-out desire to actually be separate. It's the desire to get rid of Heaven and do our own thing that constitutes a major block to Heaven. When we change our minds and that desire becomes love of Source, the barrier dissolves. The bottom line is that many still believe they can have a physical body apart from Heaven and create a place just as good. Separating from God split Heaven. Getting rid of Heaven would get rid of the guilt we feel and the fear of retribution for that heinous act.

Block 2:
We Love Our Bodies!

Whether we blame Adam and Eve for their decision or we take responsibility for rubber-stamping the choice between Heaven and Earth, we are 'glad' they did: we have bodies! Even though having a body is temporary, like a good movie, it's great fun. If you are reading this book, you know that we all chose bodies. The fact of the choosing is forgotten and obscured. The choice was made and our idea took on a life of its own. The idea of separation, now referred to as Ego, then split into millions and billions of bodily forms. The choice can be undone, but the blocks work against that. We would have to really want to choose again and systematically remove the blocks.

The creating of bodies was a free-will choice, the wanting of something different than Paradise, to know what It knows. The Ego has projected into so many bodies and other life forms, so as to never be held responsible for the "terrible crime" of not wanting to be in Heaven and destroying Oneness.

We have since discovered that we really like these "meat suits," and we identify with them. The body is now our home, and losing it would make us "homeless." It may not be perfect, but we really don't remember being in Heaven. We have forgotten what Heaven is Really like.

We like the drama, the story of our life, the special people we love, and how exciting it can be to be in love, have sex, eat good food, and live in nice houses—or not having those things. It seems like a dream at times. We are grateful for a convenient memory, forgetting about the "bad old days" of perfect Oneness in favor of the good old days of being a human being. Since this world is different from Heaven, it is a place of scarcity and survival and not having everything forces us to seek after everything: love, survival, peace, clothes, shelter, and a long list of other wants and needs. The journey through life keeps us busy seeking answers. The uncertainty of it all is an attractive feature of being in a body We love all of it, especially if it is contradictory and insane because we love drama, either watching it or living it.

We love our body identity so much that we can't imagine letting it go. We fervently hope that if there is a Heaven, we can take our bodies with us when we go there. We believe that we will need our bodies in Heaven. Otherwise how would we recognize our dearly departed family members, and how would they recognize us?

We recognize that the body isn't always pleasurable. It does offer the hope of pleasure, which is occasionally achieved. More often, the body provides pain and suffering, especially as one ages or as the result of vigorous activity or accidents. Stress and emotions can also trigger physical pain, but we still hold out for the possibility of something better. When we are sick, we hope to get well. When suffering happens, we take pleasure in blaming it on God for "making us this way" or for causing the sickness or death. Many people say that suffering is good because it causes us to value the good times even more. Our bodies make all of this possible.

Self-indulgent pleasure seeking is one of the most common reasons for loving the body. With it, we can play games, on either an individual, group, or even a national level. Some countries have had feuds going on for millennia. Often the original reasons for the fighting are long gone, but the fighting continues because many people just like to fight. Soldiers, warriors, and athletes of all kinds are heroes in most social traditions. We often think these "games" matter, that it's important who wins or loses. The games we play are fun at many levels, even those normally thought of as traumatic. We can't do all of this without a body.

Block 3:
We Now Believe We *Are* Our Bodies

We have gone far beyond just love of our bodies. We now *define* ourselves as bodies. Many think that when their bodies die, they will be gone, too. Our story, our likes and dislikes, our gender, our personality, and what our body looks like define who we are. If these body preferences are gone, then so are we.

The belief that we are our bodies prevents us from looking seriously at any ideas that don't include keeping or enhancing the bodies we have and consider to be who we are. We don't even like talking about it as it scares us to our core.

There are several theories about what happens to us when we die, and some of us don't like any of them.

Perhaps our worst fear is that we will be snuffed out completely, gone with no memory and no sense of who we were. This is what appears to happen when we have strokes, dementia or Alzheimer's disease. Maybe it happens to all of us after death. Some atheists hope that they will at least continue to exist in the memory of the loved ones who have been left behind. Genealogy is popular, but none of us "remember" those we never met. Photos or names are all we have sometimes. In any case, there is nothing we can do about it, so we might as well enjoy the time we have in our bodies while we have them. If we cease to exist after death, there won't be any meaningful consequences to us individually, no matter what we do or believe.

If we just move on to another body, as we do in dreams, then our first body is gone and forgotten. We may have several dreams each night and many of them are in different bodies. This is disturbing because we are really attached to the one we have right now, in this lifetime. Whether there is reincarnation or some other kind of metamorphosis, we still lose our body and our highly-prized sense of an individual self. We may chalk up dream bodies to metaphor, but it is still not comfortable.

If we believe that this is the only life there is and after it's over, that we will be judged by a supernatural deity who will either reward us for a life well lived or condemn us for mistakes made, then life can get very complicated. If we also believe that we are our bodies, things get confusing. Some religions say that we will get our bodies back and get to enjoy extreme pleasure (Heaven) or have to cope with the extreme pain of swimming in a lake of fire for eternity (Hell). Others say that we will wind up reabsorbed into the Oneness and our lives and individuality will be gone forever.

Even if we make it to Heaven, we might have to spend eternity at the right hand of God, glorifying It. Some say they would prefer Hell because all the people they love will be there. They don't want to spend eternity adoring some egomaniacal narcissist who wants or needs eternal adoration.

The thing is, we believe we are our body, and this belief colors *every* possible conception of where we came from, what we are, and what will happen to us after we die. We don't remember choosing to enter our bodies, yet we can't fathom losing them either.

Block 4:
The Fascination with Death

One of our worst fears is the fear of death. As a consequence, there is little doubt that the world is pretty much preoccupied with death. Take a look at nearly all high-grossing popular films and TV programs and note how many feature killings or the aftermath of death. We may not know for sure what happens after death, but it's obvious that death colors all of our living days. We are crushed by the deaths of our loved ones and glory in the deaths of our enemies.

Our lives are like stories, with a beginning and an end. We make plans for our lifetime, including relationships, careers, finances, and retirement. As in any good story, there are ups and downs and surprises as well as boring periods. Most of us are partial to stories with happy endings, and we really hope and expect that ours will have one, too. Endings often usher in new beginnings, new episodes, and we wonder if that will happen at the end of our lives as well. We know death is coming as it's part of a world that changes. Most of the time we are curious, "dying to know what happens next." We usually experience a whole range of emotions concerning our own death, the death of a loved one, or the death of someone we hate. Dread, fear, and anger, maybe even hope and joy are not unusual. Guilt and depression are often associated with our personal reactions to death, too. It's hard to deny that we are mesmerized by the entire subject.

Perhaps one reason we are so captivated is that we feel guilt for the mistakes we have made in life. There is often that core sense of remorse that we share with all our brothers and sisters for having chosen to be a body. There is a subconscious fear of consequences for doing it, yet another part of us wonders if there won't be a happy ending after all. The thing is, we won't know for sure until it's too late to do anything about it and we have to die. Death is mysterious in that sense, its consequences uncertain.

It's strange that we can have such mixed feelings about death. When we are with our special loved ones, we are happy and we want the feeling to last forever. When they are in endless pain, we want their life to be over so they can escape the pain. We sometimes vacillate between wanting their life to continue forever and just wanting to get their suffering over with.

Another hitch is that even if we believe we will be in a better place after death, we often try to prolong our life here and avoid death until the last minute. One fascinating delay tactic is that some wealthy folk, who believe they are their bodies, seek physical immortality by putting their bodies in a frozen nitrogen solution, hoping their bodies someday can be thawed, cured, and their life resumed after getting cured of whatever it was that made them sick. Many seek to prolong life in the hospital, even when the few extra days may cost the ones left behind to live a life of poverty. We do everything we possibly can to be healthy and live as long a life as possible.

Suicides are sometimes an exception to this discussion, in that they seek death for some ulterior motive. Sometimes it is to escape the pain they are feeling or perhaps to get back at someone who has angered them. Death is seen as preferable to whatever else they were experiencing, not considering the traumatic effect their death will have on those around them. People contemplating suicide are seldom thinking of Heaven.

We experience a "little death" daily when we fall asleep and are "dead to the world" for varying periods of time, theoretically resting, despite the fact that our bodies are made of energy. The phrase "little death" is also used by some as a euphemism for a sexual orgasm or pleasure. It is momentary but highly sought after. The chief similarity between death, sleep, and perhaps good sex is that we lose consciousness of our five senses for varying periods of time. This loss of consciousness is usually accomplished without trauma to the person experiencing it, that is they wake up afterwards. The point is that death may not be a bad thing to the one going through it.

Death has many dimensions. We execute people who commit heinous crimes, yet we use heroic efforts to try to save others from death in hospitals. Death is glorified in events where people die to save others or to save an idea, such as the Charge of the Light Brigade or the Battle of the Alamo. Martyrdom, suicide, and euthanasia are types of deaths that elicit admiration, disgust, or sympathy, depending on one's beliefs. We even personify death, often referring to it as the Grim Reaper.

Death is a natural consequence of being born. No one escapes it. The choice of being in a body also means choosing to experience death. There are no exceptions. Death really is a part of any physical lifetime.

This fascination is recorded in Genesis 2:17: "From that tree you shall not eat; the moment you eat from it you are surely doomed to die." As we have noted, Eve and Adam ate the apple, despite this warning. As descendants of this first couple, we have all found out what death is like. Adam and Eve were evidently curious enough about death to eat the apple and find out what it and the other consequences were like.

Then there are those fascinated by the concept of the undead, zombies. How crazy are they? Do we ever really die? How about the unborn, who never really lived, but died before birth? The fascination with life and death issues is great, in all its varieties. True, fascination might not be the right word when it is our own death we are contemplating, but then many people are what might be called "adrenaline junkies," and death issues can become an obsession.

Block 5:
The Fear of Heaven

This section will seem counter-intuitive to many. If Heaven is Love and Peace, why should anyone fear it?

Perhaps it's because many of us believe that Heaven 1.0 is the punisher of those who have been bad. We are imperfect and live in an imperfect world, making mistakes probable. Adam and Eve, a metaphor for all of us, deliberately disobeyed and were warned that eating of the forbidden fruit would result in death, something unknown in eternity. To follow the metaphor, they ate the fruit and were kicked out of Paradise. Life hasn't been easy since. Many people blame Heaven when things go wrong. The inherited guilt we feel on a subconscious level feeds a fear that we will be punished when "judgement time" comes and this is what many churches teach.

If you add to that emotional/psychological mix the probability that we will not have a body any more (it died and is in the grave), then you might get an inkling as to why many people are not anxious to go to Heaven. Who wants to go to a place where everything we value will be taken from us (body, close relationships, prized possessions)? On top of that, we fear we will be punished for eternity for not being perfect. There is plenty to fear from Heaven, as Heaven 1.0 *could* make existence really miserable, much more so that we have ever experienced in a body.

This fear leads a lot of us to avoid the subject of Heaven altogether. It could be the existential fear we all carry from wanting to experience separateness from Heaven or the more immediate knowledge that we have broken a lot of commandments that could lead to eternal damnation. Depending on our beliefs, we have many good reasons to fear Heaven.

Heaven 2.0 talks about remembering Oneness. This is truly fantastic, but for some, they can only see that we lose our bodies, friends, and history permanently. There doesn't seem to be any good outcomes here and many feel trapped. Ignoring Heaven is the best that some can muster.

If Heaven is perfect and we are not, perhaps we must become perfect somehow in order to merit reentry into Heaven. We have been told the rules and we have deliberately violated them, thumbing our noses at Heaven and Its rules. We believe we deserve some kind of punishment because we chose to leave Oneness, pretend we are bodies, and continue to refuse to return to Heaven. We really don't believe we can ever be perfect, preferring to live in an insane world of disease, death, murder, and all kinds of abuse. How sick is that?

Our ego-driven doubt continues: If Heaven punishes us for our mistakes, real or imagined, then there seems to be real doubt that Heaven is unconditional Love and Peace. How could a loving Father God punish us? If He can, then maybe this kind of love is to be feared. The example of life on Earth is that love is wonderful while it lasts, but painful when it's lost through misfortune or death. It makes sense to cling to those we love for as long as we can and to attack and hate anyone who would harm our loved ones or our way of life. Attacking bad guys is justifiable because we are protecting our loved ones, our ideas and our way of life. It's especially sad and confusing when those we love turn on us and become enemies.

Holy men talk about loving all your neighbors. That's really hard to do because we believe many don't deserve it, and we don't think we can do it. Maybe we just ought to put off death as long as possible because we are pretty sure we don't measure up. At least that way we can maximize our time with loved ones, even if old age, infirmity, injury, poverty, accidents, and horrible weather often make it tough.

There is even a "fear of God" Wikipedia article. This fear is counted by some as the "foundation of wisdom" and as a "gift of the Holy Spirit." It's "living in respect, awe, and submission" to a deity. Whether its fear of "getting in trouble" or "fear of offending God," it's still fear and not something consistent with any real part of Heaven 2.0. Perhaps there is prudence in fearing infinite power, but it's hard to see it as a "gift."

Another reason for fear, of course, is the belief that if we don't obey the laws and rules of the various churches, we will be sent to eternal damnation, forever devoid of Love and forever in pain and torment. Very few human parents would will this for their son or daughter and still say with a straight face that they love them. Isn't Heaven's love perfect? Yet many people, especially religious people, say we must fear Heaven. This fear is often a prerequisite to the church belief system.

One of the main reasons for war is disagreement on religious ideas. If this world is crazy, then perhaps the creator of this world is also crazy and, as such, is eminently unreliable and should be feared. The way this world operates, you could do everything right and still wind up in Hell on a technicality.

––––––––––––––

The blocks to Heaven are very effective in keeping us focused on the physical world. Whether they are mostly distractions or squirrel-chasing about things that do not really matter, they are effective in preventing much change unless one is really motivated. Most of us have come to accept life as it is, finding that there is enough goodness in the world to justify putting up with the evil that regularly tears it all down. We try to make this a better world and fix the problems created by the Creator. We believe we are free, unlimited, and happy. Or not. Yet many seek to remove all pain, sickness, and harm in the world without success. It seems like there is always something going wrong. Many people have put it this way:

Life is just one damned thing after another.

These blocks are the experience of people who chose to be born in a body and something that must be dealt with if we are to move on and upgrade out spirituality to Nonduality. Body consciousness really does get in the way by focusing everywhere but on Oneness. In the next chapter, let's look in detail at how the body limits our ability to perceive All-That-Is.

It's the elephant in the room––we don't really want Heaven.

CHAPTER 4
WHY WE GET IT WRONG

In starting from scratch, we have to rethink how we determine what is real. Most people think the world we live in is reality and the only reality there is, but not everyone buys the input of our five senses as the only reality.

In fact, Rene Descartes, a French philosopher and scientist, made some observations about the physical world in the 1600s that few people ever ponder and even fewer consider might be true. One is about the five senses upon which we rely for everything we know about the world:

> The senses deceive from time to time, and it is prudent to never trust wholly those who have deceived us even once.

Descartes worked to understand the world and noted that without the five senses we would know nothing about it. He even wondered if the physical world exists at all, independently of the body. He started out with the famous statement "I think, therefore I am." After that, he took a skeptical attitude toward the world, both physical and mental:

> I suppose therefore that all things I see are illusions; I believe that nothing has ever existed of everything my lying memory tells me. I think I have no senses. I believe that body, shape, extension, motion, and location are functions.

What is there then that can be taken as true? Perhaps only this one thing, that nothing at all is certain. ...but I can't forget that, at other times I have been deceived in sleep by similar illusions; and, attentively considering those cases, I perceive so clearly that there exist no certain marks by which the state of waking can ever be distinguished from sleep, that I feel greatly astonished; and in amazement I almost persuade myself that I am now dreaming.... I am accustomed to sleep and in my dreams to imagine the same things that lunatics imagine when awake.

Most people believe that the physical world exists and they in it. It seems to be the default position. Most people go further and assume that the world is all there is because the mental or spiritual world can't be apprehended with the five senses. Even then, the physical world we can perceive with the five senses is demonstrably minuscule and totally insignificant compared to the trillions and trillions of galaxies that we also believe to physically exist in the here and now, but cannot directly see. This chapter is about finding additional perspective; it will help us appreciate the nature of Heaven and how it contrasts with the physical world.

The Physical Limits on the Five Senses

In terms of proving that Heaven exists, it's very instructive to remember that while we human beings have many physical experiences, what we experience is but a tiny drop of what there is to experience in the physical universe. You will note that our bodies appear better at focusing and keeping out information than perceiving very much at all.

Vision

There are at least three key limitations on what there is to see in the world: time, space, and spectrum. Other considerations are quantity of light and point of view. These constraints are imperfections that make it impossible to definitively say that one has seen all the evidence there is on a subject and make statements of a universal character. We can only see what is here, now. What we do see isn't very much, all of time and space considered. Upon close examination, even what we think we see isn't always what it appears to be. To illustrate this point, there are a number of artists who specialize in drawing optical illusions; my favorite is M. C. Escher (1898–1972). Take a peek at some of his impossible objects, infinities, and tessellations on the internet.

1. What About Time?

"Here today, gone tomorrow." Think about it. What happened to the stuff we saw yesterday and got so attached to? Often there is nothing left and things are very different. There may be residue or remains, but things aren't exactly the same. For starters, it's a day later. We get attached to things and then get upset when they aren't there anymore. We get attached to people and then they move, change, or die.

All the things we see fade away in some manner, somewhere in time. Some things change very fast, such as in a fire, while others seem to be there forever, especially the things we don't like. Even the stars are born and die, having their own life spans. It's a real limitation that we can't see all the stuff that has ever been, nor can we see all the stuff that will ever be. That's a lot of stuff.

Albert Einstein and other physicists talked about time and space and how they are intertwined. Quantum theory posits that our universe "pops into being" when we look at it and disappears when we don't. Car keys seem to do that sometimes. There are quite a few ideas on space/time, but the bottom line is that there has been an infinity of things to see and we have missed nearly all of it.

We see only what our two eyes can see at the one place we happen to be. During a lifetime, we see very little of what goes on worldwide.

The future is another interesting aspect of time. Does the future exist in the present? How is it that things, people, and ideas just appear, never having been there before? Do they just pop into being, as some physicists suggest, or have they always been there but we have somehow missed them?

2. Seeing in Space

The next limitation on our eyes is that we can only see what is around us. We can't see anything through walls, around the bend in the road, over the horizon, or around the world.

We know that people live all over the Earth, but we ourselves can't see the millions and billions of them. "Out of sight, out of mind, out of existence?"

When you start considering that at any given time what we can actually see in one place is a mere pinprick on a huge globe, it's clear that we see very little. Compared to what there is to see, we are limited to staggeringly small amounts.

Scientists "know" that galaxies and other worlds exist, and they can see them at night and, in more detail, with devices like the Hubble Space Telescope. They are light-years away, and during the day we can't see them at all. No one has ever seen a galaxy close up (except a few parts of our own), yet there seems to be an infinity of them out there!

We seldom pause to consider that our huge planet, some call it Gaia, is less than a pinprick in the universe. Our town is a pinprick on a pinprick, yet we have no problem making global or universal pronouncements. This book is less than a pinprick on a pinprick on a pinprick! What, then, is a pixel on a video screen? A world unseen?

The same is true on the microscopic end of things. Our bodies are made up of cells, which we can't see without instruments. We believe these individual cells together form skin, hair, eyes, and indeed all the parts of the body. We sometimes look at heavily magnified pictures of the individual cells in our body, such as from a biopsy to check for cancer. We usually take the word of others as to what kind of cells they are.

One recent estimate is that each human body has around 12,000,000,000,000 (12 trillion) individual cells, more or less, that we depend on but can't see without an instrument of some type. One wonders whose job it was to count these cells and how long it took. Odds are it's merely an estimate, a guess.

The same thing happens when we begin looking at pictures of the cells themselves, which are made up of molecules, atoms, and subatomic particles. They can't be seen with the naked eye and we assume they exist based on secondary physical evidence or mere scientific theory, proven by mathematics. What? It boggles the mind to even consider the numbers involved, much less manipulate them. We still can't see them, making it the subjective opinion of the scientist.

The net result is that there are a truly massive number of the "things" we can't see, both from the galactic point of view and from the subatomic. However you look at it, our inability to see all there is, is truly impressive.

3. The Visible Light Spectrum

There is yet another limitation, and that is, even in the time and place where we are, the light we see is very small compared to the electromagnetic spectrum that exists there. What we can see is only a tiny part of that spectrum. We know there is more because we have learned to use parts of this spectrum that we cannot see. The devices humans have invented to utilize these electromagnetic waves include radios, TVs, cell phones, lasers, Bluetooth, Wi-Fi, microwaves, x-rays, and gamma-ray knives. Check out the diagram below. It shows how little of the electromagnetic spectrum can actually be seen. (Used with permission by Victor Blacus on Wikipedia)

Notice how small the range is that is visible within the electromagnetic spectrum in our world. Using current scientific understanding, not only is the visible portion of the spectrum very small, but the human brain tends to focus on only a small part of what we can see at any given time, paying very little attention to the remainder of what is in our visual field.

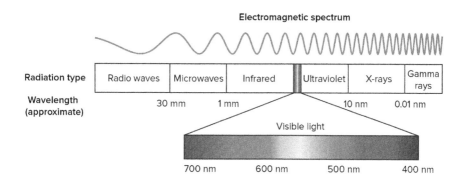

Image modified from "Electromagnetic spectrum," by Inductiveload (CC BY-SA 3.0), and "EM spectrum," by Philip Ronan (CC BY-SA 3.0). The modified image is licensed under a CC BY-SA 3.0 license

In looking at a room, we tend to look at parts of it sequentially with the middle in focus and parts of our field of vision getting more and more out of focus at its edges. If we see something with high emotional value, such as an object or person we love, fear, or hate, we might see or remember little else.

4. Quantity of Light

We are very sensitive to how much light we see. We have automatic limits for too much light (we close our eyes) and we can't see very much in low-light situations, even if what we are seeing is in that very narrow portion of the band that is available to us. A strobe or camera flash directly into our eyes can overwhelm our sight for a time, making any vision difficult until we recover. In too little light, we see poor detail and bump into things. As we age, seeing in low light becomes difficult, often leading to functional blindness.

When we do see in good conditions, our tiny corner of the world is just that, tiny. Even then, other conditions, such as emotional states, visual impairments, or cognitive handicaps, can limit what we pay attention to or remember. Lastly, we often forget what we see.

5. Point of View

Still another aspect of seeing is that we see things from a definite angle, while others may be seeing the "same" thing at the same time but from a different angle. Something may be hidden from us from one viewpoint but is more easily seen from another. An example of this is the telecasting of a sporting event. There are cameras from various points of view, and the referees are often called upon to look at various camera angles on video to determine whether a score is good or an infraction actually occurred. Sometimes they can't make out what they want to see, other times the video is the same as what they saw live. Still other times they see something different. Often it helps to slow down the replay to see it again, something we can't do in real life.

Issues arise when eyewitnesses are called on in a courtroom to tell what they saw. Many people believe that if they saw it, it must be true: "seeing is believing." There have been many studies that indicate that eyewitness testimony isn't always reliable in part because people sometimes think they see things that they couldn't have because of their point of view, not to mention memory issues and optical illusions.

Hearing

When it comes to hearing, we have most of the same problems we do with seeing—time, space, spectrum loudness and perspective. While sight deals with electromagnetic waves, sound involves mechanical vibrations that travel through the air or other media in such a way that we hear them with our ears. Hearing is the ability to be aware of or understand those sound waves. We will consider two important kinds of sound: ordinary incidental sounds and spoken language. Both are subject to the same limitations.

1. What About Time?

"Here today, gone tomorrow." Sounds seem to come and then disappear. We only hear what is going on today, right now. Sound, like light, shares this time limitation in that we can't see or hear all the things that have ever been or will ever be. No human has ever heard all trees in the forest that have ever fallen or heard all of the things that have ever been said or ever will be said. Yet we sometimes think we know everything or have "heard it all." Sounds and speech happen and then disappear, never to be heard again.

Sound has another feature: sounds must be listened to as they occur, in real time. The same sound cannot be heard later. This is to differentiate sounds that are recorded and later played back. Playing a recording is essentially a different and separate event in a different time and/or place.

Sounds, voices, and other vibrations only exist for us right now. Sounds from the past or the future aren't there anymore or yet. If we listen to recordings, they are again in the now, a distinct event from the original. Recordings of future events aren't available now. Because audio and video recordings are not the real event, they are in a different category: they are man-made and are not exactly the same as the event. Recordings can also be manipulated, introducing many more issues not germane here.

2. Limitations of Distance

We only hear those vibrations that are physically in our immediate vicinity and are of sufficient volume, neither too much nor too little. There are many other sounds going on in the world at any given time, but if they are far away, we never hear them, unless we hear them through a sound system, which technically is a separate event anyway. The sounds we actually hear are those naturally occurring in our vicinity or are brought to us through a device of some sort.

There is a distinct difference between hearing and listening. Listening is the focusing part, while hearing is merely picking up the sounds but not necessarily understanding or paying attention to them. We often hear many more things than we can listen to, filtering them out as mentioned above. Often people will swear they didn't hear something when in fact they heard it, but because they weren't listening, they don't remember it. It's as if it didn't happen if one can't remember it. We can pay attention to only one sound at a time.

There are literally millions of voices in physical bodies talking at any given time in the world outside of our immediate vicinity. Additionally, there are always voices on radio, TV, cell phones, and Skype etc. Unless they are brought to our ears somehow and we pay attention, we are unaware of them.

3. The Audible Sound Spectrum

As with light, we hear only a very small portion of the sound spectrum, compared to the sounds that are possible. The normal hearing range is between 20 and 20,000 hz, but this varies considerably. Really low frequencies or really high frequencies are available to very, very few of us.

This means that there are a lot of sounds going on that we can't hear due to the frequencies involved. Dogs can hear sounds that humans can't because their ears are capable of picking up a greater range of frequencies. Some people have hearing loss, such that their ears are damaged and can't hear some sounds due to age, loud music, or illness. There are many things going on that we will never hear, due to the high or low frequency at which they occur.

Another auditory complication is that there are over 6,000 different languages in the world, another kind of spectrum. It takes a lot of work just to learn to understand one language. It takes a long time to learn to speak, understand spoken words, read, and write a second language fluently. Hearing a language we can't understand might as well be no language at all because we won't understand it.

4. Perspective

Sounds can be interpreted differently, to some extent, depending on whether one is hearing with two ears or with one. This allows us to determine to some degree where a sound is coming from. Stereo sound is more realistic and lifelike compared to monophonic sound. Perspective can make a big difference in enjoyment, understandability, and ability to determine the source of the sound. Having two ears helps us locate the source of a sound but can be confusing since sound can sometimes bounce around, nullifying the benefit.

The content of sound can affect us emotionally and sometimes nonverbally. Words of love or hate as well as music are a kind of sound that can communicate meaning on an individual basis. Not everybody reacts the same way to words or music of any given type. Classical music might soothe some people, others will be irritated and upset. The right kind of music can heal or "soothe the savage beast," but in other circumstances, to a different person, say, someone in a prison, it can be considered a form of torture. A lot depends on one's perspective or likes and dislikes.

Touch, Smell, and Taste

The senses of touch, smell, and taste are also severely limited in terms of time, space, and perhaps quality. These three senses seem to be different in that they are much more personal to the human body and are therefore very subjective. Sights, sounds, and smells originate outside of the body, while taste and touch require physical touch perception in that specific time and place. Additionally, touch, smell, and taste seem to be more individualistic in interpretation. Touch in particular is personal because only the one person's body actually feels what the nerves are reporting, though some people believe they have sympathetic feelings. Some people have "phantom pain," that is, pain in limbs they no longer have, indicating a highly personal physical neurological involvement.

People seem to experience bodily sensations differently, even with the same or similar stimulus. One person would say a certain pillow is very soft; another would disagree. Smell and taste also vary as to whether they are pleasurable or not, often depending on whether a person is hungry and what kind of prior experiences they have had with the same or similar substances.

There is the old saying, "There is no accounting for taste." This saying applies especially to one's preference in food. People vary widely and dramatically concerning what they will or won't eat, what they love or hate in food. Smells are similar to taste in that, again, there is wide variation in preference and often no outwardly apparent reason for those differences. To summarize, one can't feel all the bodily sensations of all the bodies that have ever lived or will ever live. The same is true of tastes and smells. All sensory experience is limited to just the here and now and is highly subjective to the body involved.

Emotions frequently play an important role in the senses of touch, taste, and smell. There are positive and negative associations with these sensations that are an intrinsic part of the experience. It's true that emotions are also important in auditory and visual experiences, but they are not as apparent as with touch, taste, and smell. In any case, the senses of touch, smell and taste are all about the body. A positive or negative memory can be triggered by sensory input that becomes "associated" with that past event. This usually emotional event, whether traumatic or highly charged in some way demonstrates how sensory input is divorced from Reality and perhaps even physical reality.

The phenomenon of sensory experience complicates proving Heaven because so many people focus solely on their physical bodies. They think they *are* bodies and nothing more, despite the fact that the whole physical world we perceive with the five senses can be shut off entirely by merely falling asleep. This paradox, noted by

Descartes and many others, points to a major problem when talking about Heaven: one can't perceive Heaven directly when in a body. One explanation we will entertain is that bodies came into being specifically because they do exclude direct perception of eternity in favor of the appearance of temporary individuality.

Most objections to Heaven focus on the tiny aspect of reality we can physically perceive, seeing it as the sole arbiter of whether Heaven exists or not. If we can't see it or find it, it doesn't exist. Heaven and Earth are not compatible. Only one of them is real.

Most arguments against Heaven fail miserably when one realizes that to base the argument on the one grain of sand (our physical world) is to miss the entire beach of Reality (all the sand on the beach, not to mention the ocean or the universe). This becomes obvious when one considers the existence of everything in all of space and all of time. Looked at properly, many physicists would say at the quantum level that a grain of sand contains and is a part of all Reality, all times and places, because there is only the quantum wave; time and space cease to exist.

As we go along, you will remember that objections to Heaven are based on the physical-world mentality. It's why we get things wrong, something that's very easy to do in a body.

Heaven is really an experience. Once you have it, that is all the proof that you need. However, we are stuck using words, language, and the five senses to organize our understanding of what exactly we are talking about. It's time to take a look at definitions, since we are looking at an upgrade. Heaven 2.0 is much different than 1.0 and we need to be very clear. Calm your mind and get ready to think deeply!

CHAPTER 5
PROOF USING WORDS

In the physical world, Heaven is an abstract principle, since it cannot be demonstrated physically. On the other hand, it is easy to demonstrate that the physical world is temporary and changes all the time––it is not permanent. All-That-Is, in all its forms, together can be said to be permanent, but the Reality beyond the physical appears to be abstract. Since the world of ideas is Real, we must be clear as to what we mean when we use certain words. We must use words as symbols for this hidden Reality, despite how easy it is to misunderstand words and miss the meaning completely.

Definitions: Words Matter

You may have noted that neither Heaven 1.0 or 2.0 can be so clearly defined so that everybody will agree. Despite that, it's imperative that we come to some agreement on the meaning of certain words if we are to accomplish anything useful. Words often have many meanings; we need to focus on the meanings that will promote an understanding of the concepts necessary to understand these proofs. Certain key words and concepts in our discussion will be referred to time and again, and we must agree upon their meaning. Proving and Heaven, especially, are two of those words.

Many religious and spiritual organizations already have a definition of Heaven and our relationship to it (Heaven 1.0). It's not the purpose of this proof to say anyone is wrong, but merely to point out the need for an upgrade to our understanding of Reality if we are to clear up the issues our atheistic brothers and sisters have brought up. Perhaps we can also highlight the dead end that the physical body actually is. There are literally thousands of ideas about Heaven, and they all can't be right.

In addition to Heaven, other pertinent terms, such as proof itself, imagination, and faith must be discussed. These abstract words are not susceptible to scientific testing and we must have a clear outline how we are using these words in order to have a chance at communicating the proof.

The Term "Heaven 2.0"

"Heaven 2.0" is Life, Love, Wisdom, Peace, Nirvana, Contentment, all-knowing, all-powerful, ever-present, Rapture, Joy, all-seeing, all-hearing, eternal, Light, Source, All-That-Is, God, Paradise, everlasting Communion, ecstatic Happiness, Bliss, Eden, the Promised Land, Utopia, deliverance from all evils and lack, Wholeness, the holiest of holies, Beauty, awesome, Harmony, Perfection, changeless, better than a never-ending orgasm, beyond time and space, everlastingly creative, permanent, the "Great Beyond," Ecstasy, our eternal home, the "Kingdom Come," Life everlasting, Enchantment, Elysium, the firmament, Glory, Shangri-La, Eternity, Joyfulness, Culmination, Cloud Nine, Exhilaration, the mountaintop, Enlightenment, Euphoria, Never-never Land, Avalon, Valhalla, Beatification, Divinity, Everlastingness, the Life to come, the Celestial City, the Garden of Eden, Xanadu, perpetual Pleasure, what is fated, supreme Bliss, Felicity, the celestial regions, Transport, the journey with no distance, ambrosial, empyreal, the mythical place, Almighty God, the Fates, the King of Kings, the Lord of Lords, Providence, the Source of all Good, a better place, the good place, the Absolute, Destiny, Life after death, the Absolute Being, all-holy, all-merciful, all-wise, the Almighty, the Creator, the Deity, the Divinity, eternal Oneness, eternal Beingness, the First Cause, the Infinite, the Infinite Spirit, the Maker, the Preserver, the Supreme Being, beyond the grave, the great hereafter, the unknown, what bodes, the world to come, unalloyed Happiness, Overhappiness, Absolute Being, Overjoyfulness and the highest pitch.

Heaven 2.0 is all of these things and much more.

One of the most beautiful and poetic descriptions of the Reality of Heaven is from Kenneth Wapnick, the clinical psychologist who was instrumental in editing and explaining the book *A Course in Miracles*:

> Before there was even a concept of beginning, there is God, our Source and the Source of all creation: a perfect resplendence whose magnificence is beyond comprehension; love and gentleness of such an infinite nature that consciousness could not even begin its apprehension; a pristine stillness of uninterrupted joy; a motionless flow without friction to impede it; a vast, limitless, and all-encompassing Totality, beyond space, beyond

time, in which there is no beginning, no ending,
for there was never a time or place when God
was not.

These words just barely scratch the surface of Heaven 2.0.
The idea of a male creator in the sky, who created everything
separate and then judges and condemns some of his own
creations as no longer worthy doesn't work for most people.
Heaven is really beyond all human expression, yet we must
make the effort, for we are seeking light in a shadow world.

The Term "Proof"

The word "proof" needs to be discussed here as well. The
dictionary definitions of "proof" involve evidence, arguments,
and documentation. Essentially, proof is what you accept as
true based on your personal assessment of the evidence,
arguments, and documentation. There are, however, many
different kinds of said evidence and arguments. For example,
there are scientific, logical, personal, emotional, and historical
arguments. Evidence can be in the form of facts, hearsay, and
documentary or legal evidence. Proof is what makes sense
to you and convinces you that the premise is true. This isn't
exactly a legal forum or a philosophical argument, as they
have different standards (see Chapter 6).

The evidence proving something usually makes sense to
someone if it makes sense and fits with their experience. It's
commonly accepted that for any given proof, there will be
different opinions as to whether it's factual or believable, or
not. This lack of agreement is one of the reasons why juries

have more than one juror or "decider" hoping to ferret out the truth. If there are six or twelve jury members who agree, the probability of determining truth is more likely. Still, jurors who hear the same evidence or proof of guilt can come to different conclusions. In fact, in most trials, the lawyers for both sides believe they have proven their cases despite their opposite conclusions. It's up to the jurors to decide just which one to believe and to vote accordingly. Sadly, they can't both be right. Sometimes the truth is a casualty when there is a hung jury or a jury nullifies a law due to emotional prejudices or the skills of the lawyers involved.

In a similar vein, it will be up to you to determine which evidence or "proof" you will accept or ignore in your life based on your personal experiences. Just as juries can ignore evidence and factual proof and vote the way they want, people in all walks of life are free to ignore the evidence of Heaven if they want. Heaven may be denied or ignored, but it can't be destroyed. Ignoring the truth doesn't make it any less true.

As regards proof, the famous physicist Max Plank and others are reputed to have said,

> When you change the way you look at things,
> the things you look at change.

We all look at life through the filter of our belief systems. Changing the filter means changing our perceptions. It can go much deeper, as many believe that we create our perceptions of reality through our thoughts, beliefs, actions, and decisions. The principle is the same: if you change your mind, in time you will change your experience of life. Dr. Gerald Jampolsky wrote the famous "Change Your Mind, Change Your Life" as a way to help people do just that, though many are not willing to change their minds even with major proof.

There is only one infallible kind of proof of Heaven: your personal experience of it. Until then we must wade through multiple sources, types of evidence, and arguments. Before that personal experience, proof might be the preponderance of evidence or a deep feeling. Belief and faith are usually decisions based on all the evidence we have experienced. We then monitor and adjust that decision throughout our lives.

The Term "Imagination"

The imagination is defined in the dictionary as the part of us that forms new ideas or images or concepts of external objects *not present to the senses*. Having a good imagination means one is able to be creative or resourceful. Many have said that every action, artwork, man-made object, or concept started in the mind of somebody. It really is the premier faculty of human beings, yet science has trouble with it because it can't measure it or adequately explain it. That is sad because nearly all scientific breakthroughs have come through the imagination. All scientific experiments start in the creative part of the mind; it's only afterward that they become experiments to determine what is true.

Defining imagination is like defining creativity, you know it when you see it. Imagination is often referred to as the "mind's eye" because it allows us to transcend our physical bodies in limitless ways. Many great thinkers didn't do any physical experiments, they worked things out in their imaginations. John Norton, a history and philosophy of science professor at the University of Pittsburgh, noted that Albert Einstein's chief tool was his imagination:

> He [Einstein] used tools and methods available to everyone. He read the same text books and journals available to every scientist of his day. His principal tool was a notepad with a pen and pencil. He read and wrote and calculated and thought; and out poured his extraordinary achievements.

Imagination is best understood by illustrating it, as demonstrated in these quotations:

> Logic will get you from A to B. Imagination will take you everywhere.
> —Popular meme based on thoughts from
> Albert Einstein

> To invent, you need a good imagination and a pile of junk.
> —Thomas A. Edison

> A man may imagine things that are false, but he can only understand things that are true, for if

the things be false, the apprehension of them
is not understanding.

—Isaac Newton

The world is but a canvas to the imagination.

—Henry David Thoreau

What is now proved was once only imagined.

—William Blake

Reality leaves a lot to the imagination.

—John Lennon

Do not dismiss imagination, as it's the key to understanding
the difference between the physical world and Heaven 2.0.
It's obvious that people in a body can't experience Heaven
with the five senses. If you believe that something must be
demonstrated physically before you believe it, your world will
be very small compared to what actually is.

Everything you can imagine is real.

—— Pablo Picasso

Or, said another way, we can imagine things that are not
Heaven and therefore are unreal. We are perfectly capable
of believing our own ideas about something even when they
are demonstrably untrue. Imagination is a tool and can be
misused. Even so, we should never underestimate the power
of imagination to intuit Reality. Determining that which is
false is the key to understanding.

The source of inspiration or imagination (the terms function similarly) is an exciting topic. The word "inspire" literally means "to breathe in," implying that the idea was there already, just waiting to be breathed into the mind. Inspiration and imagination appear to be mental processes, perhaps with a strong feeling component. In a very real way, creative inspiration is at the very core of Heaven 2.0. It is the intra-communication within Heaven that requires no words, is eternal, is peaceful, is joyful, and is changeless. It is the sharing of Heaven within Itself and is on such a level that it can't be imagined in physical terms. For our use here, imagination is perhaps best defined as the mind's ability to communicate directly with all of Itself. Please remember, though, that imagination can be misused on the physical plane.

The Term "Faith"

One of the most famous writers of all time who tried to prove that Heaven exists came to the conclusion that it wasn't necessary:

> To one who has faith, no explanation is necessary. To one who has none, no explanation is possible.
>
> —St. Thomas Aquinas

That is a pretty black-and-white statement. It's interesting to note that Aquinas could point to an experience that verified his faith, not a logical proof.

Let's look a little closer. Aquinas was an Italian monk who wrote extensively on ethics, natural law, and metaphysics in the 1200s. He wrote many long, influential intellectual documents as a theologian and philosopher and is still considered a Doctor of the Catholic Church. Here is the Wikipedia account of what happened:

> On 6 December 1273 at the Dominican convent of Naples in the Chapel of Saint Nicholas after Matins, Thomas lingered and was seen by the sacristan Domenic of Caserta to be *levitating* in prayer with tears before an icon of the crucified Christ. Christ said to Thomas, "You have written well of me, Thomas. What reward would you have for your labor?" Thomas responded, "Nothing but you, Lord." After this exchange something happened, but Thomas never spoke of it or wrote it down. Because of what he saw, he abandoned his routine and refused to dictate to his [scribe] Reginald of Piperno. When Reginald begged him to get back to work, Thomas replied: "Reginald, I cannot, because all that I have written seems like straw to me" (mihi videtur ut palea). What exactly triggered Thomas's change in behavior is believed by Catholics to have been some kind of supernatural experience of God [Heaven].

Aquinas died several months later, at the age of 49, having refused to write again. His experience trumped his many years of writing about theology. We are seeking this kind of experience for ourselves, the kind that changes everything.

It's worth noting that Aquinas worked hard to understand Heaven by meditating and prayer, and it was probably this that led to his personal experience, his personal proof. Without this kind of dedication and belief, the experience probably would have been interpreted differently and probably medicated out of existence. The book he was writing, the *Summa Theologica,* was at 3,500 pages and was never finished.

As for a definition, faith is complete trust in someone or something, a confidence that things are a certain way. Some people just "get it" when it comes to Heaven. This faith might come from faint memories of Oneness, while others find Heaven to be the most reasonable of the many possible explanations of the seen and unseen aspects of life. Let us acknowledge faith's indefinable quality. Faith is also an evolving feature of human existence and is really necessary if people are to love or trust anyone or anything. Faith is like a magnet, attracting to us experiences we believe in.

Faith doesn't indicate absolute truth. It's possible that faith can be misplaced. One can have faith in science, troubled spouses, inventions, companies, or even books. When that faith is tested, and fails, adjustments must be made. New information is inevitable in life. It took a deep metaphysical experience to allow St. Thomas Aquinas to make the jump from the intellectual writing he was working on to the pure acceptance of enlightenment (remembrance), an experience that is often described as being beyond words. The purpose of belief is to be looking in the right places in order to recognize and experience what one is looking for. Very often we realize that what we were looking for was right in front us of the whole time, but we didn't recognize it. Faith must be developed however you conceptualize It. Words are merely a catalyst.

You might say that everyone has faith in something, be it tradition, other people, institutions, or loved ones. One can have faith in books and religious teachings. In any case, faith is thought to be a complex emotional and imaginative personal conviction of something that isn't readily and physically accessible to others. Faith has to do with believing in what can't be seen or proven scientifically. Perhaps it's partly a memory of past experiences, dreams, or just something that makes sense of common earthly phenomena despite contradictory evidence.

These definitions of Heaven, proof, imagination, and faith are key tools in our proof of Heaven. You will need them to follow the evidence and arguments to unblock your full awareness of Heaven as it Really is.

There are many choices of pathways to spiritual awareness and growth, but they all must come to the point of removing the barriers we ourselves have place to this growth or confusion over the nature of personal reality. It's time to see things differently, even if these ideas are different from those we had growing up. At the end of time, Heaven is the only option: there is only One of Us.

SECTION THREE
THE EVIDENCE PROVING HEAVEN

CHAPTER 6
HEAVEN 2.0 IS LOGICAL

Logic is used to evaluate arguments, which are propositions, and the conclusions that follow from them. We are arguing that Heaven 2.0 exists. All propositions are based on assumptions, which are statements that are accepted as true without proof. Such is the case here when we assume that "everything exists." Without acceptance of that assumption, there is no logical argument that can be agreed upon.

Note: Heaven 1.0 can't be proven to exist, therefore we must be clear exactly what we are trying to do here.

It's self-evident that "something" exists. Remember "I think, therefore I am"? We are part of that something, as Descartes noted, probably a mind since we use the word "mind" to label the part of us that thinks. It's an irony that even the most dedicated materialists believe in many things that they have never seen or experienced physically, even in the here and now. It's hard to even imagine all the atoms right in front of our eyes or the galaxies so situated. Yet most scientists would say these unseen objects are all proven to exist. They have no trouble believing that subatomic particles and galaxies exist, even though they have never seen, hear or touched one.

The scientific theories based on mathematics and limited direct observation serve to explain a great part of the physical world. What we are doing here is to add to that an explanation of the immaterial world of personal experience, the mental, spiritual, unseen, untestable part of Life.

A logical argument that doesn't build on material-world assumptions is a non-starter for many devotees of logical arguments. Where once physics, metaphysics and philosophy worked together, that is no longer true. Science had much success with testing, especially using new methods of observation, specifically the microscope and telescope that extended the ability to see more of the world we live in. The resultant advances in technology wowed people. Advanced math allowed more accurate descriptions and predictions of test results. Philosophy and metaphysics went by the wayside, unable to describe the unseen with such specificity.

In the 1800s many scientists began to believe that if it wasn't physical and testable, then it wasn't science, so scientists would no longer have anything to do with metaphysics or philosophy, the abstract and theoretical underpinning of Reality. The divorce worked in favor of science, as philosophy declined dramatically in popularity. Something valuable was lost: why things are the way they are and how the world fits into our lives.

One must start from agreement and build upon that. Therefore, in a sense, this book is really about building a case for our core belief, that all is one Thing, or "Heaven 2.0." Once we establish this framework of Reality, all the idiosyncrasies of other philosophies and reality descriptions can be evaluated as either temporary (false) or permanent (Real). It is very useful.

Note: This is more informal logic in ordinary language that ordinary people can understand, avoiding the specialized language that confounds modern-day formal logic.

Heaven Is Logical

Basic Assumptions

The most basic assumptions about reality or cosmology, according to many scientists and philosophers, are that it has these characteristics:

1. Universality: the laws of existence are the same everywhere.
2. Homogeneity: the universe is made of the same stuff everywhere.
3. Isotropy: the universe is the same in all orientations and all directions (the Big Bang exploded in all directions, none preferred over another) (Brighthub. com and Wikipedia).

This correlates positively with our basic assumption, that Heaven and ultimate Reality are equivalent to All-That-Exists, a single Source. It's a unity of energy that is the same anywhere and everywhere. It meets the requirements of science's basic assumptions. The aspect of uniformity is hard to assess since one can't detach from All-That-Is and objectively observe it everywhere or anywhere. It's universal and homogeneous in that the world is made of energy in some form or can be reduced to energy, or starstuff, as Sagan put it. In that Heaven 2.0 exists as a singular object with no other space to move around in, it's isotropic—there are no other directions per se. It must be the same everywhere, in all directions and orientations. Directions and orientations require something other than One to compare with and by definition there is nothing else to compare or relate to.

This book contends that the only worthy goal is to seek an unassailable description of permanent, nondual, and inseparable Reality. It's here that our belief system should rest. Permanent Reality (eternity) is simple, immutable, reliable, and beyond all imagining. Building a belief system on a temporal, changeable understanding is not worthy because it invites the collapse of understanding as those changes occur.

Dualism is based on the evidence of the body and the five senses. Since the five senses aren't always trustworthy and are extremely limited, there is a lot of room for doubt. We can only apprehend an infinitely small part of it in a tiny bit of time. Most of it can't be seen. Despite scientists' elaborate descriptions and testing of physical reality, it's still "a vast illusion," as ACIM editor Ken Wapnick puts it. The little tiny piece we can see makes us think it's all there, yet in the absence of the five senses, the entire physical world disappears. This occurs regularly during sleep or at death. In either state, who then can prove that anything physical ever existed? A memory doesn't count as scientific evidence.

On the other hand, the world of the mind never stops. It registers as self-consciousness while awake or in the dream world. There is anecdotal evidence that it exists before any individual body is conceived and continues after that body dies. Awareness of existence appears to vary by individual in or out of body, in or out of time and space. It would be logical to say that we are a permanent mind, awake or asleep, while we need a body to perceive anything physical, and that everything perceived is temporary and changeable.

Assumptions

We start with defining "All-That-Is," or Heaven 2.0 to refer to everything that exists, in whatever form it exists, the ultimate permanent Reality. All-That-Is includes the physical perceptible world, but also includes anything and everything else that might exist. It includes imagination and illusion as well as every temporary effect. This belief, this definition is found in our history, art, religion, philosophy, and emotional selves.

Therefore, our argument starts with these basic assumptions:

- All-That-Exists is just that. There is nothing that can be demonstrated to exist that is not part of All-That-Is, in or out of time and space, permanent or temporary.

- We assume that we are alive (exist) because we think.

- All-That-Is conforms to the scientific characteristics of being the same everywhere (universal), is made of the same "stuff" everywhere (homogenous, $E=MC^2$) and the same orientation everywhere (isotropic).

• All-That-Is = Reality = Life = Heaven 2.0

Using the term "Heaven 2.0" forces us to think differently about Reality. It's essentially a synonym for Oneness, or God and it's used here because it has less emotional baggage for many readers.

Inferences

1. <u>Life exists. If life exists, then all that exists is alive.</u>

Life exists since we are self-aware of being alive. If All-That-Is is universal and homogeneous and we exist, then All-That-Is is also alive and exists. "I think, therefore I am." One cannot think or "be" without being alive. By definition and the principle of isotropy, there is nothing that is not alive. Therefore, Heaven 2.0 exists and is alive, as Heaven 2.0 is a synonym of everything that exists.

2. <u>If energy exists, then All-That-Is is energy.</u>

Science defines energy as the strength and vitality required for sustained physical or mental activity or work. Living beings demonstrate this ability in the process of surviving. Some dictionaries define life as "vitality, vigor, or energy." In every case there is an equivalence, as defined and used here. Since we are alive and we think (mental energy), energy exists. Since we are energy and All-That-Is is uniform, All-That-Is can be described as living energy.

All-That-Is expresses energy in all possible forms, including light, mass, chemical, thermal, mechanical, radiant, electrical, and nuclear. Energy doesn't have to be perceptible to the five senses in order to exist, and in fact, since the body's senses are set to be so narrowly focused, the body can't perceive much at all in the general scope of things. Examples of energy not directly perceptible in any fashion by the body are x-rays, radio waves, and thoughts. There are probably some kinds of energy we have no knowledge of.

3. <u>If All-That-Is is energy and All-That-Is is alive, then all energy and its many forms are also alive.</u>

The dictionary definition of what constitutes life is inadequate in that it requires life to exhibit the ability to reproduce and to demonstrate change or growth or be organic. "Inorganic" things, ideas, and emotions are all forms of matter or energy, and are therefore alive. If everything is alive, then everything that exists is alive, including rocks, water, empty space, the Earth, etc. The concept of "death" isn't very useful either, in that it relates to physical matter changing forms, not ceasing to exist. $E=MC^2=Alive$.

4. <u>If power exists, then All-That-Is is all-powerful (omnipotent).</u>

Power and energy are similar concepts. Energy is strength and vitality for sustained activity, while power is more about the capacity to influence or force something. There is no energy or power outside of All-That-Is, so All-That-Is is invincible and can't be hurt or forced to change. There isn't the possibility of anything else to do it, therefore all power exists as and within All-That-Is. If one could conceive of something other than All-That-Is, it is false, since whatever the concept, All-That-Is would include the so-called extra parts. There is no power outside Heaven 2.0 and there can't be by the definition of All-That-Is.

5. <u>If All-That-Is is all-powerful and therefore can't be threatened, then eternal peace exists.</u>

Peace has to do with quiet, tranquility, and a lack of disturbances. "Peace" is one way to describe Reality in that it can't be threatened in any way. There is nothing to disturb its peacefulness. Chaos and violence within Heaven are merely illusion and are not capable of real activity or disturbing Heaven 2.0. The illusion of a lack of peace is perceptual and temporary, not Real.

6. <u>If All-That-Is is all-powerful, alive, and peaceful, then All-That-Is is all-loving.</u>

Love is hard to define or describe, but it can be said to be an intense feeling. It's pleasurable and would be painful if diminished in any way. If All-That-Is is truly One, and we are all part of the One, then we experience the "feeling" of Oneness, which is appropriately described as Pure Love. Any perception or illusion of its loss, such as dualism or separation from this feeling would constitute pain or a diminishment of love. In all cases, the Love of All-That-Is is really the feeling of Oneness. If we feel separate, we perceive a loss of this love. We know how we feel when a loved one dies or abandons us.

Oneness can't be destroyed or "go away," but can be ignored or denied by us.

The concept of not-Love is totally illogical as it would assert something contrary to Oneness. It would be false.

7. <u>If All-That-Is is all-encompassing, then It is all-knowing (omniscient).</u>

If All-That-Is is really all that is, then it can be described as all-encompassing, as there isn't anything that isn't part of all that is. Therefore, there is ultimately just one Knower and one thing to be known: Itself. All-That-Is is all-knowing because there is no one other than Itself to know and no one else to know about.

The appearance of separate persons or beings of any kind insinuates that no one knows everything, as only All-That-Is does so. Many assume that a separate mind is also separate from All-That-Is, but this isn't possible. The separation is imaginary and incapable of occurring, in part because there is no place separate to go to. There is no "space" in Heaven to go between anything, as space-time is an illusion that vanishes at the speed of light and All-That-Is is Light. The whole always includes all of its parts and is always aware of all of its parts, just as a human body is always aware of its parts.

8. <u>If All-That-Is is truly All-That-Is, then It is immutable and unchangeable (eternal).</u>

All-That-Is is truly the Singularity because it is infinite; there is only one Oneness. If there is nothing else, then there was nothing else to spawn it, threaten it, change it, or end it. Therefore, it can be said that It has no beginning and no end. It can't change, in the sense that Reality could be diminished or added to. The change we think we see is merely the internal functioning of creativity. The energy is permanent and cannot be created or destroyed. $E=MC^2$ does not change. There is no other "outside" observer or actor. In fact, "another Singularity" would be an oxymoron, a meaningless phrase, based on the meanings of the words. All-That-Is . . . just is.

9. <u>Since all ideas or thoughts originate within All-That-Is, it can be said that All-That-Is is creative and the source of all creativity.</u>

All ideas ever thought still exist because they can't leave their source. There is nowhere else for them to go. There is no creativity outside of All-That-Is, as there is no "outside." However, if people look at the tiny bit of the physical universe that they can perceive, they will find only a tiny bit of the creativity that exists in All-That-Is, and even that little bit is temporary. It's not unlike the pixels on a video screen: they are always changing and the image is not Real or permanent. The video screen does not change size. The creativity is in forming the images and pretending they are something else. We can only imagine the immense creativity beyond our illusory world that is permanent within All-That-Is. Eternal creativity without change is beyond words to describe or even adequately understand.

10. <u>Since Oneness is endlessly creative, all-loving, all-powerful, all-knowing, all-present, and eternally alive, experiences to the contrary are temporary illusions. They have no effect on All-That-Is.</u>

It's in this area that words and logic fail completely. The experience of time and space is the result of one impossible idea that wanted to be expressed. All-That-Is allowed separation to be experienced through denial, ignorance and temporary illusions. Its temporary dream-like quality is similar to the dreams of human beings: they appear to happen, but do not change physical reality. Temporary illusions appear to be a part of the creativity of All-That-Is.

Creativity knows no bounds within All-That-Is, with only one exception: Oneness can't be injured or harmed in any way by any idea generated by that creativity

11. <u>All-That-Is has free will because there are no other wills.</u>

Free will is the natural state of All-That-Is, as there is nothing outside of It to impede It or influence It. Human beings display free will and the ability to make choices because they are a part of All-That-Is. Each proves the other. Free will extends to and is permanently a part of All-That-Is.

At the present time, nonduality is the only system of thought that explains <u>all</u> of Reality. The purpose of this book is to demonstrate that Heaven 2.0 exists and that there is logic to support it. It is a means to an end: in order to truly understand Heaven, one must eventually experience It personally. Logic would then become unnecessary.

Those who think this view of Heaven is unique would be wrong. It has been around in all of recorded history. It's time to look at how this idea has been expressed by others for these thousands of years.

CHAPTER 7
ONENESS IS NOT A NEW IDEA

Oneness Has Always Been Remembered

The idea of Heaven 2.0, of Oneness, has never been forgotten, despite the fact that kings, pharaohs, and emperors have done their best to replace it with themselves. People went along to get along, despite personal misgivings. The kings and queens still looked like human beings, doing all the things humans do, even dying. The royals were not especially good people, either, but obedience to them was required or else punishment followed. The problem of the human tendency to personalize Deity into a personal humanoid god-figure is a sticky one and still dominates the thinking of many people. But the idea that Heaven *is* all of us (and everything else) has never gone away.

Gradually it became clear to many that there is just one power behind all of life. Evidence shows that the concept of many gods gradually gave way to monotheism. The upgrade to total oneness is being implemented as we read.

Ayurvedic Hinduism (About 3000 BCE)

The concept of just one overarching Energy is older than recorded history. The earliest writings on this concept date back at least 5,000 years, as groups of Aryans moved around Persia and India. This Heaven was the ultimate reality, the unseen principle behind all things seen and unseen. This concept, called Brahman, became a big part of Hinduism and Buddhism. It influenced many other cultures, rulers, and religions, including the Egyptian Pharaoh Akhenaton and perhaps Buddhism, Judaism, Christianity, and Islam, in varying degrees.

The ancient Vedic philosophy of northern India, in a text titled *Purusha Sukta,* describes the Universe as being spiritually One. It states that the absolute reality, Brahman, is beyond all conception and It both exists and does not exist in physical terms.

One interpretation is that the original creative wave or will, later called Brahma, projected itself into time and space. Depending on which interpretation one subscribes to, "Brahman" refers to Ultimate Reality, while "Brahma" is the Creator God (Wikipedia). The idea that people are "one appearing as many" is an expression based on this Hindu philosophy.

Akhenaton (1375–1336 BCE)

The Egyptian Pharaoh Akhenaton is often considered the first monotheist. In the *Stanford Encyclopedia of Philosophy*, in a poetic description of the sun god, Akhenaton avoids both the separation of God from the world that would characterize theism and the identification of God with the world that would characterize pantheism.

He is noted by historians because he abandoned the traditional belief in many gods and introduced the worship of Aten, the

One God. He and his wife Nefertiti are also well known as the parents of King Tut (Tutankhamen), the boy king. Tut was killed as a teenager and the followers of the old gods gradually brought back the old religion after Akhenaton's death in 1336 BCE. No one knows for sure whether the religious establishment had anything to do with ending Akhenaton's innovation, but after all, they had lost their jobs and influence. Many believe the death of his son, Tut, was also suspicious and meant to end that dynasty.

Siddhartha Gautama (563–486 BCE)

Siddhartha Gautama, who became known as the Buddha, was born around 560 BCE in Nepal, an area between India and Tibet. Few provable historical facts are known about him, but a well-known fictionalized version of his life was written to include some of the stories believed to be true. In this book, *Siddhartha* (1922) by Hermann Hesse, the Buddha was from a well-to-do Hindu royal family and tried to live a life of luxury. He later tried extreme poverty while seeking a means to end the reincarnational cycle of birth, death, and rebirth. He came to believe the goal of life is to reach Nirvana, that is, to become one with the "unborn, un-originated, uncreated, and unformed." He settled on the "middle way" and laid out the eight-fold path that would lead to the overcoming of the ego and desire, the cause of suffering.

Of note is that Buddhism spread to the Greek Empire 300 years *before* Jesus of Nazareth was born, though few Westerners paid much attention. There were Greek Buddhist scholars in Israel at the time of Jesus, and indeed the early books of the Bible were written in Greek because it was the way literate people communicated at that time.

Siddhartha's ideas and those of Hinduism were a major influence on others in the time before Christ. An example of this idea of Oneness comes from the Milesian School of Philosophy, which was founded in Turkey, just north of Israel, around 500 BCE. The Milesians believed that the whole world was formed from a single substance, which was unobservable and indefinable.

Other Greek philosophers started talking about similar ideas. Heraclitus thought the universe was governed by a divine Logos, or universal cosmic law. Parmenides, after thinking about it logically, concluded that everything that is real must be eternal and unchanging, with indivisible unity, thus "all is one."

Plato (424–348 BCE)

Perhaps the most important early Greek thinker and educator was Plato of Athens, who lived around 400 BCE. For him, the real world was the world of ideas, which contained an ideal form of everything. He proposed that the world we live in, the world of the five senses, contains only imperfect copies of those ideal forms. Plato had many other ideas, but one that is important to note here is that he didn't see the physical world as real and in fact called it the "shadow world" since physical things are but shadows of the ideal things in the real world of ideas.

The philosophy of Plato, called Platonism, and a variant, Neo-Platonism, holds that abstract objects exist outside time and space. Objects in the human world are copies of these transcendent, otherworldly ideas remembered. In other words, it was an early recognition that the source of all good ideas is what we might call Heaven today, though that term was avoided. Neo-Platonism incorporated some of the ideas of Plato and "conceives of the world as an emanation from an ultimately indivisible being with whom the soul is capable of being reunited in trance or ecstasy," according to the Merriam-Webster dictionary. Neo-Platonism is one of the philosophical bases for the Christian monastic tradition.

Jesus Christ (0–33 CE)

By the beginning of the Common Era, around the year 1, the idea of One God had gained considerable traction, especially in Judaism and Buddhism. Many believed in a person-like God, but others did not. When Jesus of Nazareth came along, many were captured by his stories and parables as well as his emphasis on love and forgiveness. His message was simple: Love God and love your neighbor as yourself. If you couldn't love them, forgive them as many times as it takes.

Jesus was among the first nondual Jewish teachers. All Jewish boys at the time received an education at home and in school, including reading, writing, and mathematics (Jesus was a carpenter.) The bible says he "grew and became strong, filled with wisdom." Then there was the incident where he did not go home with his parents, staying in the Temple for several days before he was found, "sitting among the teachers, listening to them and asking them questions. And all who heard him were amazed at his understanding and his answers." Many believe he spent time in India during the "blackout" period as the New Testament tells about his life, from age 12 to almost 30. However, as noted earlier, he would not have had to go far to find many devotees of these ideas. One striking comment Jesus made was about his unity with his source:

> But if I do his work, believe in the evidence of the miraculous works I have done, even if you don't believe me. Then you will know and understand that the Father is in me, and I am in the Father. (John 10:38, New Living Translation)

Jesus talked about turning the other cheek when people attack . . . and then forgiving them. It's pretty hard core, and this basic kind of Christianity isn't often practiced. He never said it was OK to attack others in self-defense. At the core of his story is to express love for others (our neighbors) no matter what they do to you, even if they arrest and execute you. He very dramatically demonstrated that belief when he forgave those who arrested him, convicted him on lies, and then finally executed him in a very painful way.

In the last days of his life, while Jesus was teaching in the temple in Jerusalem, some of the Pharisees heard him criticizing them in parables. They got together and asked him a question:

One of them, an expert in the law, tested him with this question: "Teacher, which is the greatest commandment in the Law?" Jesus replied: "Love the Lord your God with all your heart and with all your soul and with all your mind. This is the first and greatest commandment. And the second is like it: Love your neighbor as yourself. All the Law and the Prophets hang on these two commandments." (Matthew 22:35–37, New International Version)

After Jesus' death, the 11 remaining Apostles spread out and taught what they remembered since Jesus left no writings at all. Saul of Tarsus persecuted Jesus and the original apostles, but after an "experience" of the resurrected Jesus, he began teaching Jesus' ideas to the non-Jewish gentiles. He had his own ideas about what Jesus taught, despite never having studied with Jesus while he was alive. Paul, in his letter to the Romans, refers to himself as a slave of Jesus Christ tasked to preach the gospel. Paul had a profound and pervasive influence on the popularization of Jesus's teachings, which morphed into many sects with competing and contradictory beliefs, many of which remain today.

Plotinus (204–270 CE)

Plotinus, an Egyptian-born philosopher from Alexandria, once the intellectual hub of the ancient world, moved to Rome around 250 CE. He taught what became known as Neo-Platonism. He believed in reincarnation and the immortality of the soul as did many Christians before Emperor

Constantine the Great forbade it. He supported the idea that by working for enlightenment, one could achieve mystical union with Oneness. His writing, "The Six Enneads," were very influential on other writers, especially St. Augustine of Hippo and some Muslim thinkers.

Gnosticism (about 100-367 CE)

Not much factual information is available about Gnosticism, except as one might deduce from church attacks on it. Gnostic believers apparently had little to do with the "shadow world" as described by Plato and embraced the spiritual world as advanced by Jesus and others. The term *gnostikos* as used in Greek texts means "learned" or "intellectual." The idea of a "demiurge" is put forth as responsible for the creation of the physical world. It is similar to the idea of Ego as described by *A Course in Miracles*. In this sense, God Himself did not create the physical world, the demiurge did.

The discovery of the major gnostic library in a cave in Nag Hammadi, Egypt in 1945 brought a lot of information about the movement to light, including apostles John, Phillip, Thomas, James and Peter. These 1,500-year-old documents are all that has ever been found of a movement that was eradicated by order of Emperor Constantine the Great in the fourth century. Nondualism took a hit at this time after many tumultuous events, briefly sketched here.

Jesus taught a loving, forgiving nondual philosophy that was interpreted in many dual ways. There were many "factions" of Christianity then, even as there are many today.

At first Christianity was attacked and persecuted just like any other competitor to the official and traditional Roman Empire religion with their many gods. The Jews and Christians refused to practice the "pagan" religion after being conquered, subjecting them to ill-treatment. The Christian religion grew despite the vicious harassment.

After almost 300 years of the Romans persecuting Christians and other competitors to the state religion, Constantine stopped tormenting non-state religions (the Edict of Milan, 313 CE) and eventually took the Christians under his wing. Many historians believe it was to appease his mother, Helena, who had herself become a Christian. When Christianity was made the official religion of the Roman Empire, the treatment of Christians changed dramatically and they were no longer persecuted and put to death.

Because there were so many different and contradictory Christian beliefs, Constantine started pushing the many teachers of Christianity to get together and decide on one set of beliefs so that all Empire subjects would know what they had to believe and do. Because Christianity was the new state religion, Christians were forced to come together and agree on beliefs and practices that the entire Empire would also be forced to accept.

Many of the disagreements centered on just who Jesus was. Was he God, man, or a combination? Jesus was a practicing Jew, so some thought one had to be Jewish to follow Jesus, even to the extent of converting to Judaism to become

Christian. Many thought the world would end soon. Others were trying to figure out what Jesus's death meant. Some thought it saved everybody from the sin of Adam.

The Gnostics, mentioned earlier, saw Jesus as one who came to give people "gnosis," or the knowledge they needed to find release or salvation from the material world and enter into a perfect world.

Christian groups have been arguing with each other about what Jesus taught pretty much since his death. None of the early believers ever thought that Jesus's teachings would become the official state religion.

The Christian leaders had a hard time agreeing, and Constantine finally had to order them to determine which beliefs would become official dogma. The Council at Nicaea finally wrote down the acceptable beliefs (the Nicene Creed) and decided which gospels and epistles would be in the "New Testament."

In order for there to be just one Christianity, the emperor ordered that the written teachings of the losing groups (such as the Gnostics) be destroyed and everybody forced to believe and accept the winner's interpretations. The "winning faction," it turned out, not surprisingly, was the one from Rome and the Roman church hierarchy, pleased not to be persecuted and pleased to have their interpretation of the newly promoted religion accepted as official, cooperated fully with the emperor.

Many book burnings were held to destroy the newly "heretical" materials, including some attributed to some of Jesus' own apostles. Many of those who didn't go along with this quashing of beliefs were killed. It wasn't a pretty sight. It was a setback for the idea of Oneness in Christianity, as the newly ordered dualistic version of the religion was now enforced with the burning of books and running the newly minted heretics out of town.

St. Augustine of Hippo (354–430 CE)

Augustine taught the idea of original sin, whereby all humanity shares in the sin of Adam and Eve when they disobeyed God and chose a life separate from Him, not oneness with Him in the garden. Since all humans originated from the flawed choice Adam and Eve made, all humans since share and experience the results of that flaw. This idea does partially explain evil, as Augustine taught that Adam and Eve were given free will, even the ability to choose against God. In a sense, we are still re-experiencing the effect of that fateful decision.

Moses Maimonides (1135–1204 CE)

A Jewish scholar, physician, and philosopher, Maimonides worked to reconcile Aristotle's logic and ideas regarding science with those of religion and philosophy, believing there can be no contradiction between them, in truth. He wrote about the problems of evil, prophecy, and "true" beliefs versus "necessary" beliefs. For him, the principles of faith include the idea that Heaven exists, it is essentially simple, and it contains every possible element of perfection. Heaven is the root of everything and is essentially indescribable and complete in all ways.

St. Thomas Aquinas (1225–1274 CE)

We have told Aquinas' story earlier, but we need to include him in this section since he was so influential. St. Thomas Aquinas believed that our world did have a beginning but was created in such a way that it exists eternally.

Aquinas, who often meditated and prayed alone, wrote many intellectual books on theology throughout his life, including the unfinished *Summa Theologica* (over 3,500 pages). As mentioned earlier, just months before his death at age 49, Aquinas had a divine revelation in the Chapel of St. Nicholas in Naples, Italy. Afterward, Aquinas said,

> I can no longer write, for God has given me such glorious knowledge, that all contained in my works are as straw—barely fit to absorb the holy wonders that fall in a stable.

The *Summa* was never finished. This very powerful personal experience is a great example of faith leading to knowledge beyond all doubt.

John Duns Scotus (1266–1309 CE)

Another prominent medieval theologian/philosopher wrote a proof of the existence of God around the year 1300. John Duns Scotus, a Scottish Franciscan priest, in a lengthy and subtle proof, argued logically that there is a "first agent" endowed with intellect and will who is infinite and that there can only be one such "being."

Rene Descartes (1596–1650 CE)

Descartes said he had doubts about the existence of the physical world, yet it should also be noted that he established a firm philosophical basis for physical science. Descartes was a French, Jesuit-trained mathematician, a natural scientist, and a metaphysician in the mid-1600s. He used doubt and skepticism as tools to evaluate everything, including the study of reality, being, nature, and the limits of knowledge. He sought to establish a firm foundation for the sciences, starting with his famous dictum,

> I think, therefore I am.

He was among a number of people who considered that the physical world might be "illusory," as human senses can be deceived. He even considered the possibility that we are dreaming and that the physical world is only a dream. Ultimately, Descartes noted that there are no sure signs to distinguish between what is "awake" and what is a "dream."

Descartes is also known as the father of modern philosophy, who sought to bring to philosophy the same certainty as mathematics. He is noted for proposing that mind and body are of two distinct, separate, irreducible "substances." This distinction, from his Sixth Meditation, is known as Cartesian dualism. Descartes rejected any reliance on outer authority,

[Church or God?] an outrageous position at the time, which brought him widespread attention from other philosophers, both for and against him.

He called his approach to the world "substance monism," meaning that the world is made of just one thing. Generally speaking, there are three flavors of substance monism. The first is idealism, which holds that only the mind is real. Neutral monism says that all is energy, as both mental and physical can be reduced to energy. And the third, physicalism, asserts that everything is physical and that anything spiritual or mental can be reduced to the physical. All three approaches have been adopted by various thinkers and in various forms. There is little agreement.

Descartes is important because he was openly skeptical about the world, theorizing that it cannot be proven not to be an illusion. The physical world can be explained by science… and by dreaming. Heaven, on the other hand, can only be experienced by non-physical means.

Baruch Spinoza (1632–1677 CE)

The notion of "substance" is at the heart of the ideas of Baruch Spinoza, a Dutch Jewish philosopher who was excommunicated by his synagogue for his writings. He was inspired by Maimonides, mentioned earlier, and Giordano Bruno, an Italian astronomer who was burned at the stake because he thought that God is not separate from the Universe. Spinoza started out with the idea, not unlike Descartes, that there is only one substance, be it "God" or "Nature," and that it's responsible for everything in the universe. God "causes" everything.

All objects, according to Spinoza, whether animal, human, vegetable, or mineral, have a body and a mind, all of Heaven substance. Jewish and Christian authorities criticized his work as atheism by another name. Spinoza's idea is that Heaven not only is the world, but also is much more than the world. He saw the physical world and the mental world as extensions of Heaven, intrinsically part of Heaven, but not all of Heaven. A finger is part of a hand, but not all of the hand. The world, or finger, in this analogy is entirely of Heaven substance. It would be hard for the finger to truly understand the hand or even know of the other fingers.

Spinoza's best work wasn't published until after he died from tuberculosis at age 45 in 1677 in Amsterdam. He is credited by Wikipedia with "laying the groundwork for the 18th-century Enlightenment."

Philosophers began developing old ideas regarding God and Heaven, as science started growing dramatically. Scientists liked the idea of dualism since it narrowed their field of inquiry to just the physical, something the five senses could deal with. Others writers began to see that if they believed in an unlimited God, they must explain a lot more than just the physical world, not to mention accounting for human behavior.

Spinoza's idea that there is only one substance leads many to what is called pantheism, a doctrine that says God and the Universe are identical. This philosophy say that the Universe is a manifestation of God and that the cosmos is an all-encompassing sacred unity. The term "pantheism" was coined by Joseph Raphson in 1697 in his work *De Spatio Reali*. It was quite popular in the 1800s as many philosophers in earlier centuries had expressed pantheistic ideas, as opposed to a belief in an "anthropomorphic" God, a person in the image and likeness of mankind, separate from the physical world (Heaven 1.0).

The idea that the physical universe is God helps people justify worshiping nature or parts of it, often ignoring humanity and organized religion in the process. While it remains common, other "relativistic ideologies," such as communism and fascism, have commanded more attention.

The Catholic Church has not stood by silently as people started believing in pantheism; it attacked it, first in *Syllabus of Errors* by Pope Pius IX in 1864 and more recently, in *Charity in Truth,* by Pope Benedict XVI, in 2009. The Church fathers believe that the idea of separation between Heaven [1.0] and mankind must be protected, while ideas regarding an all-encompassing Reality (Heaven 2.0) must be stamped out.

Another philosophy developed as an alternative to pantheism and theism: pan*en*theism. Karl Krause first used this term in the early 1800s. The difference here is that there is an interrelationship between the world and Heaven, each being in the other, so to speak. Panentheism doesn't isolate Heaven from the world, as regular theism often does, nor does it identify Heaven as the world, as pantheism often does. Panentheism holds that Heaven is more than just the physical world, while pantheism holds that they are the same.

There continues to be much argument as to details, which will be addressed later in the book. Spinoza's ideas are often mentioned when panentheism is talked about. Many would say the differences are more semantic than substantive, yet Spinoza's work is important in that it reinvigorated the idea that the Divine and human reality cannot be separated.

George Berkeley (1685–1753)

George Berkeley was born in Ireland, was educated at Oxford, and was a renaissance man interested in many things. In philosophy, he was considered by Arthur Schopenhauer to be the father of idealism. He was an ordained Anglican priest and lived in America for five years (1728–1732) before returning to Oxford. Later he was appointed the Bishop of Cloyne, Ireland, serving in that post for 19 years. The University of California's Berkeley campus is named after him, as are schools at Yale University and Trinity College in Dublin.

According to Wikipedia, Berkeley developed the idea that reality as we know it is fundamentally mental and immaterial. All people are composed of mind or spirit, rejecting physicalist and dualist theories. He advanced a theory he called "… immaterialism. This theory denies the existence of material substance and instead contends that familiar objects like tables and chairs are only ideas in the minds of perceivers, and as a result cannot exist without being perceived."

Georg Hegel (1770–1831)

Georg Hegel was a German philosopher and one-time seminarian who accused mechanistic science of being too narrow and incapable of seeing anything clearly and truthfully. Hegel's ideas were called absolute idealism, as opposed to subjective or transcendental idealism. Idealism means that the physical world is a reflection of the mind, which alone is truly real. He constructed a comprehensive system of logical thought about the physical world, seeking to resolve apparent contradictions in a rational way. He believed that the increasing complexities of philosophy and science seemed to be approaching the Absolute Idea, where "all things are related and which is nevertheless self-contained." (Britannica.com)

Arthur Schopenhauer (1788–1860)

Arthur Schopenhauer was also a German idealist. He famously said that the first and irrefutable fact is that

> "The world is my idea" is a truth valid for every living creature, though only man can consciously contemplate it. In doing so he attains philosophical wisdom. No truth is more absolutely certain than that all that exists for knowledge, and, therefore, this whole world, is

only object in relation to subject, perception of
a perceiver—in a word, idea. The world is idea.

This is the philosophy from which the word "idealist" derives. Schopenhauer considered that science is really subjective all the way around, an idea within an idea. Every life form on every level is an idea. It's this kind of thinking that created a rift between philosophy and science, though Schopenhauer wasn't the only one thinking this way.

Wikipedia notes that many important thinkers have cited his influence, including Friedrich Nietzsche, Leo Tolstoy, Sigmund Freud, Joseph Campbell, Albert Einstein, Carl Jung and many others.

Ralph Waldo Emerson (1803–1882 CE)

The American poet and philosopher Ralph Waldo Emerson believed in the unity of nature. Every physical particle of nature and every mind is a microcosm of the entire universe. He believed in personal integrity and self-reliance, not in conforming to society and traditional authority, in stark contrast to most conventional religions.

Metaphysics and New Thought (1880s on)

One of the earliest Americans who might be identified as engaging in New Thought is Phineas Parkhurst Quimby (1802–1866), of Massachusetts. Quimby came to the conclusion that sickness is caused by wrong thinking and can be cured by being open to and accepting God's wisdom.

The 1800s saw a lot of change in theology and philosophy. Many old ideas that had been suppressed, hidden, or forbidden started finding audiences as they found their way into print. Universal public education was being implemented. Printing presses became more and more efficient and the cost of books came down. The idea of Oneness (Heaven 2.0) started gaining traction with large numbers of people, supplanting the idea that we are all separate from each other and from God (Heaven 1.0). As Unity, founded by Charles and Myrtle Fillmore states it, "There is only One Presence in the Universe, God, The Good, Omnipotent." Religious Science, Theosophy, Christian Science, and many other churches came from this renaissance in ancient ideas made new.

Carl Jung (1875–1961)

Carl Jung was a pioneer psychiatrist well known for his idea of the "collective unconscious," a mind that all beings of the same species share. It's a short step from there to believe that we are all One because we are already of "one mind." Jung talked of the wholeness of the collective mind and its structures. Many psychologists have taken Jung's ideas and developed them in many directions. Mindfulness is one of the many useful techniques that bears some resemblance to Jung's conceptions. While meditation has been around for millennia, Jung helped make it acceptable with those who believe in science.

Aldous Huxley (1894–1963)

Aldous Huxley, the well-known author of *Brave New World*, was considered a humanist, a pacifist, and a drug-using mystic. He was interested in spiritual subjects such as parapsychology and philosophical mysticism. He talked about how the same ideas keep popping up throughout time and space (history) in his 1945 book, *The Perennial Philosophy:*

> . . . with the one, divine Reality substantial to the manifold world of things and lives and minds. But the nature of this one Reality is such that it cannot be directly or immediately apprehended except by those who have chosen to fulfill certain conditions, making themselves loving, pure in heart, and poor in spirit.

If this idea keeps popping up throughout time, maybe that's an indication that there is something to it. It's basically the same idea that Jesus talked about on how to gain entrance to Heaven. Huxley's book does what this chapter is doing, categorizing the development of metaphysics from its rudiments in primitive peoples through the end "in the knowledge of the immanent and transcendent Ground of all being."

A Course in Miracles (1977)

Many believe that Heaven speaks to everyone and has throughout all time and all places. However, people listen to only what they want. What if someone wanted to learn a better way of life… and then began to write down whole books dictated by the "Voice of Inspiration?" There are many, including most bibles and more popular works, such the "Seth" books by Jane Roberts (1929–1984).

Arguably the best and most enigmatic is *A Course in Miracles* (*ACIM*), which takes on the task of fixing some of the errors in thinking about Heaven 1.0. The book is attributed to "Jesus," who dictated it to two New York City medical psychologists at Columbia University. It uses biblical and psychological terminology, stating that ultimately there is only Heaven and we are an inseparable part of it.

ACIM explains in detail how the illusion of separation from Heaven is responsible for the physical world appearing to come into being and that what needs to be done is to change our minds and be free of what is essentially a dream. It points out that the world is temporary and much of it is the opposite of the Love and Peace of eternal Heaven. It's similar in some respects to the "unified field theory" that science is looking for but hasn't found.

The book purposely uses biblical and psychological terminology familiar to many of the people who read it. Scribe Dr. Helen Schucman (Dr. Schucman said she is not the author; it was more like taking dictation. She was a self-described atheist at the time of the writing.) describes what the book does:

> It makes a fundamental distinction between the real and the unreal; between knowledge

and perception. Knowledge is truth, under one law, the law of love or God. Truth is unalterable, eternal, and unambiguous. It can be unrecognized, but it cannot be changed. It applies to everything that God created, and only what He created is real. It is beyond learning because it is beyond time and process. It has no opposite; no beginning and no end. It merely is.

From the preface to *ACIM*:

This course can therefore be summed up very simply in this way:

Nothing real can be threatened.
Nothing unreal exists.
Herein lies the peace of God.

ACIM advocates, in sophisticated psychological language, Jesus's message that each of us needs to look for the divinity in every person and use forgiveness of self and others as the road to the total, personal experience of Oneness. It suggests that what is important is the *experience of Oneness* and not the book or the words. Schucman notes that *ACIM* is in the format of a self-study course to discourage those who would make a religion of the teachings or use it to control others.

One of *ACIM*'s greatest contributions is to give a detailed intellectual understanding of Heaven 2.0. It has inspired many other books, speakers, and conferences on nondualistic philosophy and practice in the 40+ years it's been out. It's ironic that most Heaven 1.0 thinkers consider Heaven 2.0 as atheistic because Heaven/God is not a "person" in human terms and is not an entity separate from humanity. What should not be forgotten is that Heaven is beyond complete human understanding and that words are ultimately a large part of the problem we have in perceiving Oneness. Words come and go; Peace, Joy, Love, and Power are immutable. Ideas to the contrary are a temporary illusion, destined to disappear and "pop out of existence."

———————————

CHAPTER 8
OUR SHARED EXPERIENCE

Oneness hasn't always been our shared experience from the point of view of history in time and space. The idea of time, space and bodies in a material world was an attempt to create a separate world, away from Heaven completely. As we have noted, the memory of our real Unity has never been extinguished, though it has been hidden in plain sight, in many ways. Let's look at how we have slowly recalled that Reality, in part due to the temporary and unsatisfactory results of this experiment.

A Short History of the Memory of Heaven

Even our apparently primitive ancestors knew there was more to life than they were experiencing. A detailed explication is found in two great books, *The Case for God* and *The History of God,* both by Karen Armstrong, a former Catholic nun. Armstrong researched historical records for what people throughout the ages have believed and practiced. She noted that thinkers throughout history have noted the "mysterious power" of the universe, its regularity and order. What she called the "perennial philosophy" is the desire to be a part of this power and how many stories and rituals were modeled after it.

In her books on God, Armstrong paints a detailed picture of this "larger dimension of being" throughout the millennia. In that Heaven 2.0 is a "larger dimension," we will see that this concept has been common throughout history and still is. The words might differ, but the overarching concept shines clear. This section on historical experience is informed by Armstrong's insights and history books, as well as common knowledge and observation.

Humans have always had a concept of something greater than themselves and of the existence of a better place than where they were. This feeling and emergent ideas evolved along two tracks: one more of a physically based Heaven 1.0, the other, more metaphysical and nondual. The idea of wholeness itself has always been around, even if it's often subverted and distorted for other purposes.

Ancient Longings

Prehistoric men and women had a rough life by modern standards, working hard just to survive. Food was hunted and obtained with great difficulty. Plant-based food was seasonal, but there were usually animals that could be killed year-round. The hunter-gatherers had to spend a large part of each day hunting for, killing, and preparing food for their family group. Shelter from the weather and from wild animals at night was another survival task that consumed a lot of time and attention. Heaven, per se, doesn't seem to have been a concern early on, other than a longing for and/ or remembrance of something better.

The remains of prehistoric humans, plants, and other animals have been pored over by archeologists and paleontologists, seeking to construct a picture of what life was like for them. Many scholars think that the aboriginal peoples wondered about how to influence their surroundings and the other living beings in their world in such a way as to get their needs met. Intriguingly, Armstrong says that, in addition to recognizing that they lived in a dangerous world, there also appears to have been an emotional connection between all living things and a kind of respect for the spirits of the animals and plants they killed and ate. They tried to live in harmony with the spirit or life energy in all things, including the sun, storms, lightning, the sea, the Earth, and the stars. This is absolutely true of the aboriginal people of Australia, one of the few tribes whose ancient beliefs still survive.

There are over 340 caves in France and Spain that have prehistoric wall paintings, some dating as far back as 40,000 BCE. Some show men wearing animal masks, which might indicate identification with the animals or an attempt to use the animals' images to fool other animals or enemies. Survival was foremost in their minds, and any innovation that made it easier for people to hunt safely and successfully would have been welcomed. There are indications that people saw themselves as part of nature and were respectful both of the plants and animals they ate, which they realized would soon become a part of their own bodies.

At some point, clans and tribes started appointing one of their members not only to think about these things but also to collect and preserve the knowledge and experience they had acquired. Trying to figure out why they sometimes had good luck and sometimes bad was important. When it was bad, people died.

When someone got sick or injured and died, an important resource to the group also was lost, not to mention the impact of the grief of those who loved that person. Somebody needed to know what to do to help a sick or injured person recover. The development of the shaman was important to the survival of human groups. Inept groups, it's thought, died out.

One very interesting interpretation of the cave drawings is that humans didn't see themselves as permanently man or animal. One could become the other. In the sense that they ate each other, it was undeniably true on a physical level. The personalities of people varied, and some showed similarities to the ways animals behaved, demonstrating a possible kinship. The wall painters apparently believed that people had a connection with certain animals and friction with others. Many early humans cherished animal companions and guardians, as many still do today. Some archeologists think that there was a kind of inner communication between humans and their companion animals that helped both to survive and thrive. Some people believe they have an inner communication with animals even today. Horse, dog, or cat whisperers are examples.

It's also thought that when hunters found it necessary to kill an animal, it wasn't without some discomfort, because they were killing something not totally unlike themselves or something they might become someday. Even today, there are many vegetarians and pet owners who feel this connection and communication. For them it's not easy to "put down" an animal friend even if it's suffering. Many of today's hunters feel a connection with their prey and are careful to hunt only what they can eat and use, with a sense of admiration and gratitude to the animal that gives its life for them. Unhappily, there are some for whom this isn't the case.

Many people celebrated the circle of life, aware that someday, after they have died, their bodily remains will also be consumed by other living things, becoming food for the kind of animals they ate. The circle has been a continuing theme throughout history. A circle is a line without an end and is a symbol of oneness.

The practice of animal sacrifice also has a long tradition, including in biblical times. While today it's thought to be barbaric, thoughtless, and mean-spirited, it apparently wasn't thought of that way originally. Armstrong says our ancestors lived in difficult times for both animals and people. Survival was hard work and often painful. In this world, death was thought to be a good thing, an end to the struggle to live. On the other hand, the people were grateful and they honored the animal that allowed them to live by giving them its body. It was a reminder that something good awaits all of us at death. It was also a recognition that human life depends on the destruction of other lives, both plant and animal.

One of the earliest concepts of Heaven was that it's a "good place" where life wasn't a struggle.

Many Gods

It appears that as populations grew and changed, especially through the development of agriculture and better food-storage methods, people had time to think about more than just surviving. It was natural to look at life and notice patterns, trying to determine what is responsible for establishing and guiding the rhythms of life. People would look for the spirit in living things, the nonphysical essence of everything.

The rudimentary idea of this larger dimension became *person-ized* for many people. There seemed to be many forces in the world, and some thought that there might be many individual unseen spirits/gods who might be in charge of things like nature, lightning, the Earth, the seas, etc. The anthropomorphic instinct in humans is strong, creating everything or anything in our own image. The unseen Heaven was no exception.

Since there is a natural tendency for people to try to influence each other to get what they need, it was probably an easy step to try to influence those "unseen spirits" or gods that seemed to control or alter their lives. If one could control the unseen causes of the weather and other natural phenomena, then life would improve dramatically and give them a feeling of some control and thereby a sense of confidence in the future.

Societies realized that some people were better at some things and not so good at others. Shamans were appointed who showed that they had skill in divining and influencing the unseen part of life. They developed expertise in the use of plants and other natural remedies to aid in the trances they would enter into and often induce in their patients for healing. They were frequently successful in helping their patients recover, but not always, to be sure. The shamans knew the gods, who to call on, and how to proceed. Many of the plants (and derivatives) that they used are now used by modern doctors and pharmacists.

Early Greek and Roman history and even the Old Testament are filled with references to the various "local gods." Their ideas about the unseen were the inspiration for many stories, prayers, entertainments, and instructions. The gods were popular as an explanation of why life was the way it is and spawned whole new approaches to the spiritual world. The concept of Heaven or gods as persons lends itself to stories about how things came about. Not everybody believed in many gods, as we will see soon, but shamans and others found the stories to be useful in changing the behavior of others. In difficult times, when societies started wars to get what they wanted, they prayed to their gods for help.

Development of Religious Bureaucracy

It's self-evident that some religious leaders figured out a way to take advantage of these beliefs not only to help the whole community but also to ensure a comfortable place for themselves.

Apparently, the gods became not just an explanation of life, but also an industry of its own. A visit to places such as Delos and Delphi in Greece or the pyramids and temples in Egypt demonstrates how closely intertwined the worship of the gods and commerce became. The kings and pharaohs often portrayed themselves as gods, and the priestly caste evolved and cooperated to mutually meet the physical needs of all concerned. They had learned how to make a living from the religious thought and beliefs of the people, beliefs the priests fostered.

Here is an example of how things worked: The ruler and priests would decide that they needed a new temple and/or palace. They then solicited donations (taxes) from the people in order to curry favor with the gods by building a temple in the god's honor. The commercial interests provided the materials for and the construction of what the gods-king-priests wanted, which the people's money paid for. The builders were paid well to construct temples to honor the god and house the ruler-god and/or the priests. The ruler and priests did their part, interceding with the gods on behalf of the people, while the people worked to pay the taxes. Everybody was happy in good times, not so much in extended bad times. The people got blamed for not giving enough in bad times, when they didn't have much. The religious always asked for more donations to keep up the good times or to try to reverse things in bad times.

Lives then were short. It was assumed that the priestly class was "in the know" on how to avoid bad after-life consequences. After all, that's what the literate priests told the general non-reading working people. Books were handwritten and very expensive. While the names and the concepts of Heaven have changed somewhat, this self-sustaining alliance of religious, ruling, and commercial leaders is still common in many societies. It's difficult to tell where earnest belief stops and dedicated self-interest begins in many organized religions.

To be sure, the combination of religions, government, and business contributed to the spread of spiritual ideas. The net effect was positive, promoting prosperity and a sense of certainty among the various nations, even if the groups often contradicted each other. It's perhaps also one reason why religions are loath to change things: no one wants to upset a system that has worked so well for so long.

In any case, the collective belief in Heaven remains. Many studies, including a relatively recent one by Dr. Roger Trigg, a research fellow for the Department of Theology and Religion at Oxford University in the United Kingdom, demonstrate that it's human nature to believe in God and the afterlife and to see purpose in everyday life. This belief prevails even after centuries of the dominance of science in intellectual life. Trigg's study, *Cognition, Religion and Theology Project*, a study of studies, shows that belief in God or Heaven is pretty much a universal tendency, especially in children. This is the evidence of the "where there's smoke, there's fire" variety.

There is little agreement on the details of the belief in God, but most of us believe that we come from a loving Source and that we shouldn't be hateful to our fellows or overvalue physical things. The longing for this belief is a very strong type of evidence. This chapter has demonstrated that the memory of a better place remains despite systematic efforts to undermine and subvert it.

CHAPTER 9
INSPIRED WRITING AND MUSIC

There are many kinds of inspired art that give a glimpse of the Divine. There is far too much to cover here, so here we will focus on just a few examples of the kind of writing that can help people find subtle evidence of Heaven 1.0 and 2.0. Words from beyond seem to flow into the consciousness of those willing to listen quietly. Sometimes these words seem to emanate from a great place, based on the motivating content and a feeling of euphoria. Inspired music is beyond the scope of a written book, but often the lyrics can also be special. A key is how they make you feel—relaxed, peaceful and loving. In this chapter let's look at examples of overtly channeled books, near-death experiences, poetry, novels, and music lyrics that serve as a guiding light for many.

Those Who Come Back to Tell Us

The conventional wisdom is that nobody has died and then come back to tell us about it. Or do they, often?

There are many books described as "channeled" – dictated to a scribe by folks who were once alive in a body. Many of the books of the Judeo-Christian Bible are described as "given" by God: that's another word for having been channeled. The Muslim Quran is described as being channeled to Mohammed by the Archangel Gabriel. If that's possible, then dead people or angels, with the help of the living, can write books. Some say it isn't possible, but it happens all the time. Bibles are just the most well-known and best-accepted examples, though we seldom think of it in those terms.

Many bookstores have a section for channeled works, written by people who have once lived and come back to pass on lessons learned in cooperation with a living writer. If a person dies, that is, their body dies and their spirit moves on into other "realms" of the Universe, why would it be impossible to whisper into the ear of a willing listener, still alive in a body? In Heaven 2.0 we are all part of Oneness: there is a direct connection between all minds, with or without bodies. The fact that there are so many such works is evidence that "the dead" can and do come back to tell us about it. They do it all the time and are limited only by the willingness of living people to listen.

Channeled books aren't any more reliable than those written by living authors. Some are pure trash, channeled by confused spirits; others contain wise and sage advice. The point here is that there is evidence of the survival of the human spirit after the physical body falls apart. That immediately expands the definition of what a person is, beyond time and space.

There are many books purported to have been written by Jesus, angels, and other enlightened entities. Our purpose here isn't to judge them all, but to point out that they do exist. Evaluating them is simple but not easy: if they inspire love, joy, peace, and similar emotions, they are valid and useful. If they inspire division, judgment, violence, or hatred, they should be avoided. Some of the best, in addition to the Bibles of the major religions, include *A Course in Miracles, A Course of Love,* and *The Way of Mastery.* Valuable books are any that inspire a person toward remembering, forgiving, and loving.

In the Christian Bible, Jesus commented that we should be aware of "false prophets." This advice can also be applied to channeled books as well as other modern teachings. His metaphor was twofold:

> Beware of false prophets who come disguised as harmless sheep but are really vicious wolves. You can identify them by their fruit, that is, by the way they act. Can you pick grapes from thorn bushes, or figs from thistles? ... Yes, just as you can identify a tree by its fruit, so you can identify people by their actions. (Matthew 7:15-17, New Living Translation)

He said it's OK to be skeptical at first, because initially there isn't any way to know where channeled teachings come from. Confused material is common. After careful consideration, one should try to get a feel for what effect the material has on the listeners or readers. It should be fairly clear fairly soon.

Siddhartha Gautama Buddha is reputed to have said something very similar, in this very liberal translation and now an internet meme:

> Do not believe in anything simply because you have heard it. Do not believe in anything simply because it is spoken and rumored by many.

Do not believe in anything simply because it is found written in your religious books. Do not believe in anything merely on the authority of your teachers and elders. Do not believe in traditions because they have been handed down for many generations. But after observation and analysis, when you find that anything agrees with reason and is conducive to the good and benefit of one and all, then accept it and live up to it.

In every case, we are responsible for what we believe and how we put ideas into practice. Channeled writings are important because they are evidence that humans survive death and Heaven is very real. They are very, very strong evidence, and the feeling of Heaven can be very powerful when personally experienced. Avoid material that makes you feel uncomfortable.

This book is the result of personally channeled material over many years.

Near-Death Experiences—Those Who Come Back to Tell Us, Part 2

In the previous section, people who were once dead found a way to channel information to those living in this "shadow world." There is a second way to get information from "the other side," by going there temporarily and then returning to the very body one left. Again, this happens all the time in accidents and hospitals. A person goes into a coma or a state of unconsciousness and the body shuts down and is clinically dead. Sometimes it's spontaneous and sometimes the return to full consciousness is medically induced. It's very easy to find books and movies about individuals who have personal experiences of Heaven. The mystical experiences many seriously ill and injured people have had while in a coma or otherwise blacked out are now available for others to read about or watch. This type of personal experience proves Heaven in the strongest way possible while in a body, to that person. It's not surprising that one must get the body's sensory apparatus out of the way to do it.

There have been a lot of studies by medical doctors and others on near-death experiences. It's fairly common for a person who has clinically died and then later revived to report having seen people they love who died a long time ago. Examples include people in hospitals who suffer cardiac arrest and technically die—the heart has stopped and there are no brain waves. Hospital revival efforts bring them back to life, regaining a beating heart, brain waves, and consciousness. Near-death experiences are also often reported after people wake up from long periods in a coma.

Near-death experiences were brought to popular attention in the book *Life After Life* (1975), by Dr. Raymond Moody, a medical doctor and forensic psychiatrist. An estimated 20 million copies have been sold describing remarkably similar experiences of patients who have died in accidents or in the hospital and were later resuscitated.

People who experience being brought back to life often don't want to talk about their it because they believe they will be thought mentally ill. It could be that their belief system filters out a lot of their experiences, much as the dreams of the average person are forgotten mere minutes or seconds after waking up. The human body is not geared to experiences beyond its limitations and is set up to forget things it doesn't believe in or doesn't want to believe in.

Those who do remember what happened after clinical death and subsequent resuscitation often tell a story about a light, meeting deceased family, and a renewed faith in their work on Earth, love, the value of a return to physical consciousness, and a plan to fulfill their life intention or purpose.

Moody started by collecting stories involving near-death experiences in his practice in the 1960s, eventually publishing them in *Life After Life*. These experiences suggest that the individual mind or entity survives physical death. Moody lists the common stages of a near-death experience:

1. Hearing odd sounds, such as buzzing or tones.
2. Having a feeling of rising above the body.
3. Feeling peace and no more pain.
4. Having an out-of-body experience.
5. Having a feeling of traveling through a tunnel.
6. Reuniting with relatives who are no longer alive.
7. Meeting a spiritual being, such as an angel or Jesus.
8. Seeing a review of one's life, usually very rapidly.
9. Feeling a reluctance to return to life in the body.

The fact that so many people have such similar experiences without their five senses functioning would seem to indicate that the body isn't necessary for life or consciousness to continue. Moody says it doesn't provide "conclusive proof" of surviving death, but it's suggestive of that.

Near-death experiences often strengthen a person's belief in Heaven. To a person who already believes in Heaven, it's experiential proof of something they already believe in. On the other hand, someone who doesn't believe in Heaven might be induced to reexamine their ideas about death, since the "nothingness" they anticipated did not occur. Usually the intensity of the experience is one of its main features.

Scientists who believe that the mind and all spiritual phenomena are the epiphenomena of the brain point out that people who report near-death experiences have not actually died, but that depends entirely on how one defines "death." The real issue is that these people's records usually show clinical death, followed by resuscitation. Some scientists believe the experience is essentially a hallucination. Near-death experiences usually occur when the person is clinically dead, when there is no brain activity. If there is no brain activity, then the question remains, how could it be a brain function? Most other hallucinations occur while people are physically conscious and there is plenty of brain activity.

People have the ability to create fantasies, shadow people, and even hallucinatory worlds to fill physical emotional voids in their lives. People in solitary confinement in prison or stranded in caves, islands, or on boats develop an imaginary, perhaps hallucinatory world to help them survive. If people have this ability, isn't it possible that this whole world we live in is also an illusion, albeit a shared hallucination? We definitely have the ability, according to scientists, psychologists, and mediums.

Many people have also had the experience of being guided to safety by an "unseen power" when in a serious accident or dangerous situation. This experience is often proof for that person of the existence and guidance of Heaven.

People who have had near-death experiences, such as the famous and respected neurosurgeon Eben Alexander who wrote *Proof of Heaven: A Neurosurgeon's Journey into the Afterlife*, say their experience of Heaven was very strong. Alexander genuinely believes that he went there, despite being predisposed to try to explain it away in scientific neurological terms. It's the meaningfulness of the experience that provides the greatest evidence, topping years of academic study and clinical work.

Poetry

Often, writers are inspired to express insights they have received in ways that illuminate the human quest to discover who we are. Poets are often the most successful in communicating these ideas. The thought of an all-encompassing Heaven 2.0 is fairly easy to find in literature, constituting evidence of a personal nature that it exists.

This is one example, from poet William Blake's *Auguries of Innocence:*

> To see a world in a grain of sand,
> And a Heaven in a wild flower,
> Hold infinity in the palm of your hand,
> And eternity in an hour.

Blake (1757–1827), a British poet, painter, and printmaker, looked deeply past the dream and intuited that since all is One, one can find all of it in anything, anywhere. There is only one "thing" and nothing else. How brilliant to take such a big idea and embed it in just four lines! It often takes an artist to express the nearly inexpressible. That is the power of inspired art.

One can find many poets, artists, and photographers inspired by Heaven 2.0 at such internet venues as:
- nondualitymagazine.org,
- livingnonduality.org, and
- nonduality.com.

Novels

Science fiction and fantasy novels are also popular media for nontraditional ideas about reality. Their many stories are made into movies that hundreds of millions of people see. They exercise our imagination, often exploring tragedy, evil, and death. Our heroes or antiheroes are people with superpowers or machines with super capabilities. Oneness is not often a theme, but the stories help loosen the bonds on our imagination and perhaps the memory of "a better way."

One striking example is Robert Heinlein's cult classic from the 1960s, *Stranger in a Strange Land.* One of the main characters, Valentine Michael Smith, was born on Mars, the son of the first astronauts to get to Mars. The astronauts died, and the native Martians raised Smith. Twenty years later, a second expedition brought him back to Earth, where his learned skills fascinated many.

Valentine was in full control of his mind and body and was very sensitive. He could "grok" things without words, "grok" meaning to:

> understand so thoroughly that the observer becomes a part of the observed—to merge, blend, intermarry, lose identity in group experience. It means almost everything that we mean by religion, philosophy, and science—and it means as little to us (because of our Earthling assumptions) as color means to a blind man.
>
> ——various sources.

These advanced mental and spiritual abilities captured the imagination of many in the 1960s and '70s. They reminded us of the abilities that the saints displayed, especially their psychic abilities and skill in seeing Heaven in other people. Valentine equates life with Heaven in a very pure way. He is troubled by war, clothing, and negative emotions such as anger and envy: subtle yet effective.

There are many books that talk about time travel and other abilities that stretch our understanding of what is possible. Video games are often in the form of a challenging journey and in many respects, mimics a good book, except that the player gets to determine the way the plot unfolds. Sometimes a wise person is portrayed in ways that can illuminate an aspect of our journey to understanding and remembering.

There are many books and movies that are themed around the experience of life after death, including *Heaven is Real*, *Stairway to Heaven, Five People You Meet in Heaven, Heaven Can Wait*, and the classic *What Dreams May Come*. The Internet Movie Database (IMDb) lists around 40 movies that deal with the afterlife. These movies resonate with large audiences, and this resonance and the experiences of those who have had near-death experiences are very powerful evidence of the existence of Heaven.

There are a whole host of non-fiction books specifically about nonduality that might be characterized as philosophy, spirituality, self-help, or fantasy. An internet search will demonstrate how many there are. One, Joan Tollifson's List of Recommended Books lists well over 100 contemporary books on "nonduality and waking up." Those who are interested in learning more have many choices to get more information.

Music

Music is another powerful form of art that can reach past the mistaken intellect and induce and deepen meditation and prayer states. Hymns and songs that speak to people in a positive way and songs that tell a story can be persuasive and can stimulate many emotions, even ecstasy, a state reminiscent of Heaven.

Here is an example of a classic art-rock musical group that talked specifically about the illusions of reality with glimpses of Heaven. In the Moody Blues 1967 song "Nights in White Satin," drummer Graeme Edge gets right to the point at the end of the song, in his "Late Lament":

> Red is gray and yellow white,
> But we decide which is right
> And which is an illusion.

Another Moody Blues song, "The Land of Make-Believe," is more direct:

> We're living in a land of make believe
> And trying not to let it show.
> Maybe in that land of make believe
> Heartaches can turn into joy.
> We're breathing in the smoke of high and low,
> We're taking up a lot of room.

Many of these songs work on more than one level: first they describe the love two people feel for each other, second, the love that binds the universe together.

Ultimately, as the Moody Blues pointed out, we all have to make up our minds regarding what is an illusion and what is Real. Everyday life can get boring and tiring because of the sameness. We are enamored of new illusions, but they never seem to go anywhere. We get tired of illusions that are seemingly endless—and ultimately pointless. Many have arrived at this same conclusion.

A classic in this vein are the lyrics in a song by the Eagles, "Hotel California," (written in 1977 by Don Henley and Glenn Frey), which refers to the situation we find ourselves in. Some see the evil in the world and think constantly about the "dark side," the flawed idea that lured us into the dream of physicality in the first place:

> And she said, "We are all just prisoners here, of
> our own device."
> ...
> "Relax," said the night man,
> "We are programmed to receive.
> You can check out any time you like,
> But you can never leave!"

There have been literally millions of personal insights shared by storytellers, writers, musicians, playwrights, painters, sculptors, weavers, craftsmen, architects, and other kinds of artists throughout time. Their very existence is wonderful prime evidence that the Divine continually and constantly communicates through receptive individuals who have experienced the loving inspiration of All-That-Is in a way they can understand and express. The key to hearing these messages is listening and watching for them.

CHAPTER 10
MINDING THE MIND—WHO WE ARE

Let's try to remember who we really are, as we are the best evidence of Heaven 2.0. If all is One and One is eternal, then we must be a part of It. Eternity is thus our home and we have never left it and we never really can. Whatever else we think we are, we must agree that we are or have a "mind."

While the body has limits in time and space, the mind can think about the past and the future in addition to the "now," regardless of the body we think we live in. Mental limits are only those that are self-imposed or accepted from others. The mind is electromagnetic (think EKG), and the body and anything material is also electromagnetic (think quantum wave and subatomic physics). Whether we create our own reality (Heaven and I are One) or we believe that something or somebody created us, we are all made of the same stuff, energy. There isn't anything other than energy that we could be made of, mind or body.

Thinking about the mind has its drawbacks. The mind itself can't be observed; there are no pictures and few diagrams as to how this might work, but we will do the best we can.

New Thought followers Charles and Myrtle Fillmore founded the New Thought Unity School of Practical Christianity in 1889, and they thought long and hard about what people are. Charles expressed some of his observations in a book entitled *The Twelve Powers of Man (1938)*. While not necessarily religious, it expresses a keen observation of what people are capable of. The 12 powers are:

1. Faith
2. Strength
3. Wisdom
4. Love
5. Power
6. Imagination
7. Understanding
8. Will
9. Order
10. Zeal
11. Renunciation
12. Life

Fillmore taught that each person has these faculties and can use them to live a more fulfilled and centered life. Since there is only one Mind, these characteristics are in all seemingly separate people. You can find out much more about these characteristics elsewhere. We mention them here because they are a detailed description of the multi-faceted mind which we are and All-That-Is is.

Some scientists consider our sense of self, or mind, to be an epiphenomenon, or a secondary byproduct of physical brain activity, they believe that "we" are merely incidental to our bodies running around on Earth. An epiphenomena commenting on other epiphenomena begs a lot of questions, including just how it all started or how that works. Which came first, the brain or the epiphenomena? It would be more accurate to say we *are* a mind, rather than that we *have* a mind. After all, it's the mind that has a sense of self, it's not like keys in our pocket, something we have. Bodies do not have a sense of self-consciousness without the mind.

Those who say that our minds were created along with our bodies have a problem. There is no definite evidence of beginnings and endings to minds, only that of bodies.

In fact, there is a lot of subjective evidence that the mind exists before physical birth and survives physical death. Most people, under hypnosis or even spontaneously, will have reincarnational memories, suggesting being alive in a different body prior to birth and again after the death of the current body. Many people experience communication of a sort with incoming or outgoing minds, either spontaneously or with the aid of others, such as in séances or channeling. Minds don't seem to have beginnings and ends in the same sense as the body does.

One description of the mind is that it is a type of organized energy, not unlike the quantum wave. Remember that science has concluded that energy can't be created or destroyed. The same must be true of a mind; it might change, yes, but be destroyed, no.

There appear to be few limits on the mind, other than those that are self-imposed or accepted from others. There are an infinite number of ideas about the mind, yet the mind can't be physically or objectively observed. We think, which is by itself evidence that we and Divine Mind exists.

Some people want to split the mind into spirit and soul, considering them to be different things. There is little or no evidence that this is so, only arbitrary definitions as to what is a mind and what is a spirit or soul. You could say that a mind is an aspect of spirit. Others say that the mind is the part of us that is aware of physical experience, and the soul is the part that is eternal. In any case, the terms refer to basically the same thing and most definitions are purely arbitrary and nonfunctional. Still, there are a multitude of theories regarding the mind.

Some people can actually see mental energy around a person, calling it an "aura." Others can see bands of energy, negative ideas, sickness, or other emotional states reflected in the colors of this energy field. It's debatable whether these perceptions are mental or physical. There is a lot of evidence that can't be explained in physical terms.

If all minds are actually joined, then it's an excellent explanation of all kinds of psychic phenomena, such as telepathy, hypnotism, apparitions, hauntings, clairvoyance, precognition, psychokinesis, near-death experiences, reincarnation, and other personal events. There are many scientists researching parapsychology, consciousness, and meditation, all aspects or activities of a unified mind, not unlike Jung's theory of the collective unconscious. It helps explain how some can read other people's minds, something that would be impossible if there wasn't a connection.

Who are we really? We are all one with All-That-Is with no literal separation. Heaven 1.0 says we are all separate entities, separate from Heaven. That is why an upgrade is needed. Perception is not Reality; perception is illusion. Words will never do justice to Oneness, but we do find clues everywhere that point us in the right direction.

Astrophysicist and cosmologist Carl Sagan spent his life trying to explain esoteric physics in ways that people could understand. He said that on a physical level we are made of the same stuff:

> The nitrogen in our DNA, the calcium in our teeth, the iron in our blood, the carbon in our apple pies were made in the interiors of collapsing stars. We are made of starstuff. (on *Cosmos* TV program)

What if the starstuff he was talking about is energy and merely a temporary manifestation of the mind? Heaven 2.0.

Dictionaries define mind as self-consciousness or awareness, memory, will, feelings, attention, and/or intellect. There really are a lot of ways of looking at ourselves and our abilities, and it would be extremely easy for this discussion to get hopelessly lost in the weeds of terminology and frames of reference.

The bottom line is that we can confidently say we are "a mind." "I think, therefore I am." We can also say that there is no apparent barrier between minds and that a more accurate description is that we are all part of one huge mind. There are many manifestations or interactions that aren't physical and that have no other explanation. With this mental unity in mind, let's move on to examining other aspects of the functioning of our minds, facets such as inspiration and imagination, free will and love. These characteristics will deepen your appreciation for just who we are and what the mind really is: part Divine Mind, Heaven 2.0.

CHAPTER 11
CREATIVITY

Heaven is creative. Evidence of creativity is evidence of Heaven; if All is One, there can be no other source. The permanent Eternity, Heaven 2.0 is endlessly creative. Sometimes this creativity goes by other names in the material world, such as survival, art, science, sports and many other human activities.

It is sometimes difficult to understand creativity due to its pervasiveness. Very few things stay the same in the physical world, and change seems to be a constant. A lot of the creativity seems to be aimed at mundane activities and doesn't seem spiritual at all, yet it is a mental/spiritual ability. The confounding thing is, from the point of view of the material world, that the material world seems permanent and the spiritual is unseen. The reality is the opposite: the "spiritual" world is permanent and the material world is temporary. The creativity of All-That-Is is amazing.

Our physical universe of duality is like a temporary file on a computer. It was imagined and created, served a purpose, and then erased like it never was. If it were to be kept, it would get in the way and perhaps cause problems. This illusion of a world is here to show and demonstrate that Heaven cannot be broken into duality.

The problem is that those of us reading now are still working with that temporary file, this temporary world. At some point, we realize what we really want is what we have in Heaven 2.0. Most people believe in Heaven and are trying to figure out how to return: the purpose of this book.

People throughout history have intuitively known or been taught that if they enter into a prayerful or meditative state, they can receive guidance or inspiration. Most find the activity and the process helpful and continue it throughout their lives, especially when times are difficult and guidance is needed on how to proceed. Those who pray and meditate believe in this communication channel. While this is all "anecdotal," it is evidence of Heaven. You could say that all of the temples, churches, mosques and other houses of worship are concrete evidence of the belief in Heaven and how to relate to It.

That alone is amazing creativity. Let's look a little deeper at this process of shaping our future and getting our needs and wants met. It is a cooperative undertaking that is used by most people, day in and day out.

Inspiration and Imagination

Imagination is our creative ability to change the world or ourselves to solve a problem or express thoughts and feelings. Inspiration is getting motivated to make those changes. The word "inspiration" is from Middle English "to breathe into." It was understood that when Heaven did give guidance, it was experienced as a breath into the mind. Inspiration is usually experienced this way, an idea that just pops into the mind.

It happens all the time, with inspiration experienced in response to asking for guidance of some sort. The inspiration may not be immediate and one may have to be patient. Many would say it was inspiration and imagination combined. For some, it is a voice, for others it could be a feeling, an image, or music. It's hard to define, but relatively easy to recognize in retrospect. The urge to do something or make changes can lead to immediate action. Artists, writers, musicians, architects, and many others collaborate with the Divine knowingly or unknowingly through their creative process. There are so many kinds of inspiration and guidance and they are experienced in many different ways.

Inspiration and imagination are usually the just the start of a mental and physical process:

> Genius is one percent inspiration and ninety-nine percent perspiration.
>
> —Thomas Edison

> When your heart speaks to you about what you need to do to sustain life on this planet, listen to it, make a difference, and be an inspiration for generations to come. Be inspired by people like Gandhi, Mother Teresa, Rosa Parks, Martin Luther King, Christopher Reeve, Albert Schweitzer, Helen Keller, and many others.
>
> —Bernie Siegel

Many philosophers say the very creation of the universe was through the power of the imagination, not just "evolution." The world may have popped into being, but it was created. The impetus for the "Big Bang" came from somewhere. First there is the entire world of perception, the galaxies, planets, the oceans, flora and fauna, the cells and molecules right down to the subatomic world. The very complexity of the human world is further evidence of the energy behind imagination: people, buildings, roads, cities, libraries, electronics stores, music collections, and art galleries. When you take into consideration the mental and social aspects of the world, it really is a testament to the creativity being expressed by and through people and to the inspired idea that is responsible for the world in the first place.

Those who believe neither version of Heaven exists usually consider it imaginary, a "figment of our imagination." What is a figment anyway? It's something that "exists in our imagination and we believe it to be real, but it doesn't exist in the real world" . . . yet. By this definition, most great ideas were once figments that someone believed in long enough to find a way to birth them into the material world of form. It's a matter of timing, belief, courage, and even perseverance. Whatever created the world is infinitely creative and imagination is one of its chief tools. To say that something of this immensity and complexity is merely a figment of our imagination seems ludicrous, yet it once was. The physical world is governed by cause-and-effect and the cause of the world is the creative power of inspiration and imagination.

The human process of creativity starts with inspiration and imagination. It is evidence of All-That-Is, of which they are a part of, by definition. It's hard to discuss creativity in Heaven 2.0 because we have deliberately blocked most of what we remember, but it is easier to look at our temporary world and get some clues. If there is only one Reality, even the temporary thoughts must reflect their source, as there are no other patterns out there to copy.

Illusions

We have often used the word "illusion" to refer to the temporary world we live in to differentiate it from Heaven 2.0, which is permanent, eternal and essentially immutable. To many, the word means just an idea and not real. Despite the fact that this world feels fairly solid, it can be caused to disappear by merely falling asleep. No one can deny that change is a hallmark of this earthly existence. We talk about its beginning and scientists and preachers conjecture about its end. Our bodies are made only to experience the temporary world and for this reason, many do not believe that the permanent unchanging Reality even exists.

This could be because people really enjoy illusions and prefer them. We discussed this in some detail in the blocks to the awareness of Heaven in Chapter 3. Illusions are a manifestation of a creative ability that could only come from their Source. There are many uses of illusions within the illusion that both entertain and prevent serious consideration of waking up. Sometimes there is a misuse of illusions, yet because they are illusions, they don't really exist. They waste time, yet time doesn't exist in Reality either. Still we dilly-dally within this illusory world.

We all seem to love to be entertained by the illusions and dreams of others. We love to hear stories, watch movies or TV, the fantasies of other people. We seek them out. We often become emotionally attached to all aspects of these illusory worlds within the world: our bodies, family, parents, brothers, sisters, friends, workplace, grocery stores, and electronics stores, all mixed in with Superman, Batman, Star Wars, Star Trek, Harry Potter, Halo, Minecraft, Pokémon, and many others. The characters in games, movies, books, TV shows, and songs stimulate us physically, visually, audibly, and emotionally, yet these characters are demonstrably not real people. But real people love these characters and have real emotions when they think about them and/or experience the entertainment medium they are in. Reality and illusion are blurred.

The body doesn't care; it is a tool and it drinks it all in, no matter what the source of the illusion. Experts say that some parts of the brain can't tell the difference between a movie and reality. We cry in parts of some movies and are measurably startled during scary ones. It's the frontal lobe of our brain that helps us keep on track, if it hasn't been disabled with drugs, alcohol, or mental illness.

Our technical brothers and sisters are getting better and better at making illusions more "life-like." Computer animation is now at the point where computer-generated images look almost exactly like traditional photography, and in fact, it's hard for most people to tell the difference. Films have been made using the moving images of dead actors appearing in new roles. In any case, "seeing" should not necessarily be "believing." Movies are illusions where we willingly suspend belief and view the story as if it were "real." The technology to create "virtual reality" is progressing exponentially; it can literally fool people into thinking they are somewhere where they are not. If they get really good at it, one might not be able to tell the difference between the physical world and the VR world. After all, we can't tell that this world isn't real until we learn to realize that it's temporary. Yesterday is gone forever.

Even this illusion is an illusion: what we seem to see isn't always what is there. For example, printed materials are the perfect demonstration of how something can be incomprehensible on one level and we can turn it into something else on another. A magazine or newspaper photograph is made up of little dots on paper when we look at them very closely, yet from a greater distance we see a whole and smooth image. TV screens and computer monitors are made up of dots as well, called pixels. If you get far enough away from either printed or electronic media, the dots are merged by the brain to form a relatively seamless picture, but nowhere is there a truly smooth, seamless image except as it's interpreted in the brain.

The little dots of our electronic gear were inspired by the physiology of our eyeballs. Light enters our eyeballs and strikes 120 million photo sensitive rods and six to seven million cones on the retina, which in turn sends electrical impulses to the brain. That alone is evidence that the mind/ brain is intrinsically involved in the process of seeing. Our head is an ultra-, ultra-high definition light receiver turning little pieces of information from the retina into a seamless image in our brain. That is creative!

Someday soon we will realize that just as there aren't real people in the video, that there aren't any other people in this world; it's an illusion and there is only One of Us. Hints are already showing up in books and movies. One recent example is *The Matrix* and its sequels. The issue is that we have chosen as humans to consider an illusory world as permanent and real and continue to choose to treat it as such. It's an error in thinking.

The world of illusion is the world of perception, a recognition of something other than self and the world of projection, the placing of feelings onto others and creating new apparent worlds, all to avoid experiencing Oneness. It's very creative, but:

> There is no truth. There is only perception.
> — Gustav Flaubert

> It used to be, everyone was entitled to their own opinion, but not their own facts. But that's not the case anymore. Facts matter not at all. Perception is everything. It's certainty.
> —Stephen Colbert

These are examples of creativity being used to not see Heaven 2.0, the Real World or All-That-Is. Perception and projection require another person to function; it requires what cannot be. That is the beauty of the "temporary file" because it allows us to see what separation would look like if it were possible. You get to choose how long you enjoy the dance of more than one and the blame game that goes with it. When you are tired of this tiny seemingly endless and pointless game, you can clear your mind of temporary file illusions and go for looking at the world in a different, more Realistic way:

> If the doors of perception were cleansed, everything would appear to man as it is, infinite.
> —— William Blake

After all, we do have free will.

CHAPTER 12
FREE WILL: MAKING CHOICES

Free will is defined by the Cambridge Dictionary as:

> The ability to act and make choices independently
> of any outside influence.

Free will is an aspect of Oneness and having it is evidence of our being part of All-That-Is. The physical universe and our physical bodies are the result of a free will choice.

Free will does not mean the ability to change Reality. It only means that we can choose freely from available choices and one of those choices appears to be a dream or illusion of what it would be like IF separation could occur. Separation is neither possible nor desirable, and we are exploring that choice, exploring this idea in the form of the physical world.

Free will is one of the most creative abilities we all have and we know it from our earthly experience. With a human body in a world where survival isn't certain, one must make choices almost continuously on what to do, what to say, where to go, with whom to mate, even how to treat people who are evil. The entire world is a creative experiment in the use of free will, from the beginning to the end of time.

In any case, the ability to make choices seems to be built-in and is indicative of our Source. Since we have free will, our Source must also have free will; it had to come from somewhere. If we are part of our Source, then free will is also an aspect It. The one choice we can't make is to separate from the whole, no matter what. Eve and Adam thought they did, but it never happened. Genesis said Adam fell asleep. Paradise was still there, but Adam began dreaming of existence separate from It where life and death, good and bad appear to reign.

To follow that metaphor a bit further, this entire world, all of it, is Adam's Big Dream. We inherited free will and can continue dreaming the dream of a world discrete from Heaven. We remain in the dream until we choose to wake up. Free will is honored; we are experiencing separation without it Really happening. Thus, you can say this world was created through free will and will end only through free will. Any waking up will have to be of our own volition.

We don't want to remember our choice to experience separateness, yet that choice resulted in this illusion, a dream world, often a nightmare of thinking we might actually pull it off. Our plight in this self-made world is like the old Greek myth of King Sisyphus of Corinth, who "was punished for his self-aggrandizing craftiness and deceitfulness by being forced to roll an immense boulder up a hill, only to watch it roll back down and having to repeat this action for eternity." (Wikipedia) No matter how hard or how long mankind tries to roll the boulder of separation up the hill and make it real, it won't work. We can remain in the fantasy world we have created, or we can do something else. We do have the ability to undo our choice and awaken from the dream, if we want to.

People seem to do what they want. Sometimes the choices available appear to be unlimited, other times it might be the "best bad choice." We make our decisions based on what we think will be best for us now, even if we don't really know what that is. We decide to go along, or not, with the situations we find ourselves in. In any given situation, some people wait for inspiration before acting, others take the easiest way forward. We have the ability to choose.

People are often confused by the situations that confront them and do not know what to do to insure a good outcome. Often choices are made without taking the consequences into consideration and often those consequences are not known to the chooser: a double whammy.

Free will doesn't mean that we are free of the consequences of our choices, which may be different than what we thought they would be. Often, we make choices to do something we really want, only to find out that other unforeseen things come along with them. When exercising our free will, it's the hidden parts, the parts we didn't bargain for that seem to make or break the happiness or acceptability of these choices. Free will isn't as simple as it might appear to be on the surface.

Many people believe their lot in life is the result of the choices they make throughout their lifetime. It's one way to account for the many unique people and situations that arise in life: different choices made in different times and places. Some choices are easy, others are difficult. Sometimes we feel compelled to make certain choices. At other times death or financial ruin are the only alternatives to some choices, but even then, the choices are there; not all choices are equal or beneficial. If we don't like the choices, we don't have anyone to blame other than ourselves.

Even in the death camps of World War II, people had the choice of how they viewed their situation and, in limited ways, whether to help others in the same situation or not. The book *Man's Search for Meaning,* written by Austrian psychiatrist and Holocaust survivor Dr. Viktor Frankl, is one of the best books ever written on this topic. Even in extreme situations, Frankl demonstrated that people have mental and emotional choices even when physical choices are restricted. He taught that free will extends to the meaning of life and the choice to find a reason to keep on living.

Here is an illustration that might help illuminate some of the problems with the concept of free will on Earth. A person walks down a road and comes to a T intersection with a wall preventing them from going straight. How many choices are there? Perhaps three: stopping and doing nothing, going to the right, or going to the left. Those are the obvious choices. A person might be able to imagine more choices, such as flying away, digging a hole and going under, climbing over the wall, or even walking through the wall as if it wasn't there.

Not all choices are really good. Some have negative results, others are impossible. Some are obvious and some have negative repercussions. A lot of choices are heavily influenced by biological imperatives, instinct, habit, or compulsion.

Our will might be free, but the choices may not be "independent of outside influences." Free will also includes the ability to make very bad choices with bad outcomes. To the extent that "free" means no one forces us to make any particular choice, that seldom applies in the human experience of the material world. Ego sees to that. There are so many "forced choices" caused by other people, circumstances, or just the element of time. Some choices need to be made immediately without thinking or consulting. Yet we always have the ability to resist or to go along with these compulsory choices. Even then, a person can always choose their attitude in any given circumstance, said Frankl. Decisions made by following your feelings, experience, or inner guidance are more likely to have good outcomes.

It's very easy to overthink free will and use it as an excuse to justify evil and attack someone. If we perceive anyone as evil and try to destroy them, we have forgotten that they are a part of our One Self. Therefore, to attack others is akin to a dog chasing its tail; the only one that gets hurt if the dog is successful and bites his tail is the dog. If we are all One, hurting anyone else is hurting our Self, a losing proposition. The only way to destroy evil is Love.

We have met the enemy and he is us.

–Pogo

The Zen version of "free will" is that the only way will becomes free is when it is One with the will of our Source. As always, the choice really is ours and it's never too late to make the right choice.

CHAPTER 13
THE SEARCH FOR LOVE

Perhaps the greatest evidence of Heaven 2.0 is the search for perfect Love. Let us never forget that a synonym for Heaven is "Love." In a very tangible way, we are looking for that indefinable something beyond words that can only be found in who we are, but can't be found permanently in the dream we have created. Love can be talked about, but it is helpful only when it is experienced or expressed.

Love Makes the World Go 'Round

Living in separation from Heaven makes us crazy. Not only do we think we are separate from our Divine Source, but also from each other. Separation is what we chose, but it really is an intolerable situation and one of the first things we began searching for, our intrinsically connected nature. It is perhaps this feeling that makes us feel empty inside, seeking the Oneness, the connection we've always had. With that feeling, everything is great; without it, life is lonely and depressing.

It's hard for some to distinguish just what love is in the world, as there are at least two dozen definitions of "love" in some online dictionaries. Love of a parent and child is different from sexual love, which is different from the love of brothers or sisters or a generalized love of one person for humanity. For some, love is sexual intercourse, while for others it's a concern for another's well-being. Words have a very hard time defining or limiting love and the many ways we feel

Oneness within. It's a very real feeling and is at the core of any feeling of pleasure with or without a body being involved.

Love can also be displaced onto physical things, places, causes or a number of other non-human subjects. It is often called desire, but its root cause is the search for Real Love, which melts away issues. Buddhists are right when they suggest that losing desire is necessary for spiritual progress.

A Course in Miracles addresses this central focus on love by saying that all human interaction revolves around expressions of love . . . or calls for love. A murder or a sexual assault is a call for love. The tender embrace of a loving couple is an expression of love. It's all about love or a perception of its lack in our life.

Most religions are about loving Heaven as our creative Source. Sometimes it's hard to tell if the love of God is pure, nonjudgmental Love or just a plea for help when things go wrong in our physical world.

Many people express love for some of their family and friends, but no one else. This limited, specialized love is more about loving just a few people. If you love just a few, it means not loving the rest, about whom one doesn't care for or perceives as an enemy. It's a part of the call for love and an attempt to keep up the illusion of separateness, not remembering Real Love for All. It's as if our special love for those we like is more important than the unconditional love we should feel for all people in the universe. It can be a knotty problem, but doesn't have to be.

Love is perhaps the strongest motivator of human activity, and it's certainly built into our physical bodies. Ego, the idea of a self different from Heaven, uses this strong power to create more apparent individuals. Sexual attraction and intercourse are necessary for most babies to be conceived, perpetuating the species and expanding separateness. More sex equals more babies equals more separate individuals.

To a body, sexual climaxing, or orgasm, is one of the most pleasurable feelings one can experience in life, outside of drug-induced feelings of ecstasy. These temporarily heightened physical sensations are highly sought after. Perhaps one of the reasons that so many people drink, do drugs, and have sex, is because it subconsciously reminds them of the pleasure of Love, the enjoyment of Heaven. We have forgotten the massive, pure pleasure that is associated with our being in Heaven, forgotten after our decision to experience separateness. Not all sex is good and many people will take what they can get, in hopes of more.

Many, many books have been written about love, sex, drugs, and the seeking of pleasure. Our intent here is to point to this universal desire as evidence of our desire for and existence of Heaven itself, the Source of all love. Suffice it to say that in this world there doesn't appear to be enough love to go around and people do many crazy things looking for it. Pure love is found by waking up and remembering we have it all. It's the goal of almost all religions.

Jesus is quoted in the Christian Bible as saying the way back to Heaven is to love God with your whole heart, mind, and soul and to love your neighbor as yourself. It has less to do with whether you like the person or not, but more with how you treat fellow human beings. Following the prompts of Love and expressing love to all you meet, whether they are special to you or not, is a way to find more love in your life and perhaps find all the love you all seek: The Love of your Creator. After all, if we are all One, then real Love exists in all of us and in everything. It takes a while to figure out which are the false parts of the illusion, ignore them, and see the parts of our illusion that are Real Love.

Again, just the fact that we think about love in some fashion most of the time is an indicator that we need Love. We look for it in our lover, our family, our social group, and our larger society and country, even our world. Many of us see ourselves as a part of the human family, sharing much more than just DNA and a planet. While you can spin it other ways, Love really is evidence of something more than just a chemical reaction or biological imperative.

> If someone thinks that peace and love are just a cliché that must have been left behind in the '60s, that's a problem. Peace and love are eternal.
>
> —John Lennon

Consider the powerful feelings and capabilities we all have, whether we use them or not. We don't often look closely at ourselves or our potential. Inspiration, imagination, free will and love are just a few ways of looking at ourselves. Remember Charles Fillmore's 12 powers? If they are in us, they are in the greater One, only without self-imposed limits. Going within to meditate, pray, or find peace are practices we can all use to remember that we chose our way in and can chose our way out, with help from our Loving Source, who gave us the breadcrumbs we need to find our way out, even as we were going in.

CHAPTER 14
SCIENTIFIC EVIDENCE

Bread Crumbs

Science is a wonderful way of determining how things work. It is not so good with what they would call the supernatural. From a nondual perspective, this world is an illusion and much ado about nothing. Finding evidence within the illusion is difficult since the purpose of the illusion is to hide Reality. That is why science concerns itself mostly with the physical and observable universe, trying to operate within strict parameters so that its results are reliable and useful. From the material point of view, Heaven 2.0 is not directly observable, testable or repeatable.

We have already noted the basic assumptions of science in Chapter 6 on logic about reality or cosmology: universality, homogeneity, and isotropy. A University of California, Berkeley website, however, lists three more assumptions basic to the building of scientific knowledge:

1. There are natural causes for things that happen in the world around us.

The site says that the natural world includes "all the components of the physical universe—atoms, plants, ecosystems, people, societies, galaxies, etc., as well as the natural forces that work on those things. Elements of the natural world [as opposed to the supernatural] can be investigated by science. Human beings have natural causes by this definition.

The physical world is assumed to be a "cause and effect" world: everything that happens has a cause that can be determined. When things change in a changeable world, the studies become less useful. Change your mind, change the world.

2. Evidence from the natural world can be used to learn about those causes.

This means that evidence can be determined from experiments and observations of the natural world at a specific time and place. Piles of data is thus generated in the effort to learn about why people do what they do.

3. There is consistency in the causes that operate in the natural world.

This assumption is problematic because it is so general. In the pursuit of Truth, this is more about describing some human activities in the material world accurately. The physical sciences seek to find the laws that govern nature, while the social sciences and other newer branches are more descriptive of activity rather than immutable laws. In our efforts to prove Heaven, there isn't much here that is helpful, partly as we have already noted, science eschews anything spiritual or religious in any way.

Quantum Physics

Many scientists would not agree that quantum physics is physical evidence of Heaven 2.0. That is in part due to our discussion of just what Heaven is and the antipathy of science for spiritual matters. However, our definition of Heaven 2.0 as an infinite All-That-Is, is very similar to what the quantum field is and how scientists describe it. We must take some license here, but the fact is that if Heaven exists, you would expect to find something like the quantum field. Part of the problem is that most physicists don't want to draw comparisons since they don't believe in Heaven 1.0 and so they often go to great lengths to avoid doing so. When mathematics and physics reach concepts like infinity, the discussion ends abruptly.

Theoretical physics is similar to theology in many ways, in that the quantum field, the space-time continuum, particles, wave theory, and other stuff can't be viewed with the naked eye or even a high-powered microscope. From a material point of view, these things are ideas, part of a belief system and not concrete in the same way as a paved road. In many respects, theoretical physics and spirituality are similar in that they can't be directly seen, heard, or felt and much of what the scientists say must be accepted on faith, that is, believing in things unseen. Physics does have a ton of mathematics to support it. We will pass on mathematically defining the quantum field because it's infinite and no one can observe or measure it, making it similar to All-That-Is.

Historically, when tools such as magnifying glasses and microscopes came along, scientists noticed that many physical objects were made up of other, smaller objects. There is a long history of trying to break down objects into their smallest part (atomism), trying to find that which can't be broken own into anything smaller. The new instruments confirmed that general theory and the trend continued. The scientific progression of big to smaller now goes something like this: physical object, cell (if alive), molecule, atom, subatomic parts (electrons, protons, neutrons, etc.), and finally a whole zoo of other particles with cool names like quarks and charm. Finally, there is the quantum field, which is infinite, and is at once packets and a wave. The packets could symbolize matter and the wave is pure energy. There are many scientific experiments going on, and new descriptions and theories are forthcoming.

Definitions of the quantum field vary, but charming ideas such as wormholes, black holes, singularities, and other concepts have entered the collective imagination. What the quantum wave is, exactly, is theoretical at best, but most physicists see it as at the core of physical reality, in much the same way as we see Heaven as core reality. As long as we are "trapped" in a brain with limited perception, Reality will be difficult if not impossible to describe much better than it already has been.

Science describes a piece of wood, metal, or living flesh as not just a physical object but as electrical energy, or, one of my favorites, "potential."

It's also described as "waves" at one and the same time. Light behaves both as waves and as particles. Light also behaves differently depending on whether it's being observed or not. These particles are not unlike small children: they behave differently when they know someone is watching them. One common internet description of light is

> ... little tiny mass-less particles called photons. Photons are basically just little tiny bits of stuff that fly through the air in straight lines.

There's a lot of conjecture here, but the particle/wave duality is intriguing. One logical deduction from this theory is that we and every part of us and everything that exists are part of the quantum field. We are truly a part of this quantum "All-That-Is." This is a major piece of evidence, and it's so simple that it's profound.

William of Ockham, a medieval theologian, conjectured that with competing explanations, the simplest one, or the one with the fewest assumptions, is the best. The idea that all is energy and everything is only one energy wave, known as the quantum wave, is at once simple and compelling. The quantum field isn't easy to view or test and is more in the realm of theory, mathematics, and spirituality.

This general observation and others have led many theoretical physicists (but not all) to describe the quantum field, where all this stuff happens, as resembling the behavior of thought. The thing is, there is only *one* quantum field. This is the place where "all is one." That means it's also all of us all the time and in everything around us, all the time. This is essentially our definition of Heaven 2.0: Divine Mind.

If it interests you, there are many books that describe the intimate relationship between physics, philosophy, and spirituality. Just Google it.

The Higgs Boson (2012+)

The God Particle: If the Universe Is the Answer, What Is the Question? is a 1993 book written by Nobel Prize–winning physicist Leon Lederman and science writer Dick Teresi who led the search for a subatomic particle that some describe as the uncuttable particle: the "God Particle." The atom was once thought to be that fundamental uncuttable particle, but subatomic particles changed that view.

The Large Hadron Collider, beneath the Swiss-French border near Geneva, Switzerland, was built between 1998 and 2008 to test and search for the old "God Particle," also known as the Higgs boson. The Collider is 500 feet underground and about 17 miles in circumference. The main purpose of the collider is to fire protons at other protons at extremely high speed as they enter the Compact Muon Solenoid, a huge magnetic cave about 70 feet long and 50 feet in diameter, with many sensors. Data is collected by computers, collated, with particles showing "signatures." Sometimes new particles can be "inferred."

The existence of the Higgs boson has been proven using this equipment, but not everybody accepts it as proof of God's existence. One problem, of course, is the definition of God. A boson is an elementary particle with zero spin that follows a statistical description given by Satyendra

Bose, an Indian physicist, and Albert Einstein. It's said to prove the existence of the "Higgs Field," which is part of a mathematical explanation as to how elementary particles gain mass in the physical world. Other explanations will probably be forthcoming.

Some believe there is no such thing as an "uncuttable" particle. There is now new research into something called the "sterile neutrino;" it is now being referred to as the new "God Particle."

Some scientists say the nickname "god particle" is misleading and it is the news media that calls it a proof of God. Is it important? Yes, but let's keep it in perspective. Think for a second: no one has ever seen an atom, much less subatomic particles. Special devices such as the huge Compact Muon Solenoid are needed to have any visual representations of the atom at all. Since the scales are so vastly different, it's impossible for the human eye to actually see the Higgs boson. It's almost all mathematics. And the current research is geared toward figuring out a more precise mathematical model of the nucleus of an atom and how it's held together so that it feels solid. We already know physical things feel solid and some may not need that detailed of an explanation.

Still, science says we're looking at a world made of subatomic particles, which make up atoms, which make up molecules, which make up matter, which makes up inanimate stuff and animate cells, cells that make up bodies, plants, and other living things, which make up the world we live in (along with rocks and things like that), which, along with the other planets, makes up the solar system, which, along with other solar systems, make up galaxies, which make up. . .??? It's a perfect description of how Oneness is split infinitely to the extent that Oneness can't be found by any of the five physical senses or mathematics, the very definition of duality.

The Higgs boson is also still a theory, an idea, a belief that may help, but it isn't something anyone is likely to experience personally. The "sterile neutrino" and its significance has yet to be determined. In any case, only a few scientists will really understand the evidence and higher-order mathematics involved. Even fewer will say it is evidence of Heaven 2.0.

A Non-scientist's View of Scientific Evidence of All-That-Is

A lot of science and physics is now all about higher mathematics. The following is a fascinating example of what that looks like and how it can be understood differently. Combining science and art is something of an oxymoron for most people. After a production of David Auburn's *Proof*, a 2001 Tony Award and Nobel Prize–winning drama and movie, one critic said of the play:

> It's a wonderful drama that elegantly describes the world of mathematics, and suggests how ill-suited the mathematical notion of truth is for life. It's impossible to divine the future, and it's no easier to derive it. We're only as certain

as our next best guess. (Daniel Rockmore, *Chronicle of Higher Education*, June 23, 2000)

Director Andrew Denny had large panels constructed for a San Antonio production of the play, upon which were written these formulas from Einstein's Theory of Relativity:

Let F = the reference frame, V = velocity, M = mass, and E = energy.

Given: kinetic energy = $1/2\ mv^2$.

If $1/2mv^2$ is the kinetic energy of M moving at V, then the net energy (E^1) of M in this frame of reference (F^v) would be $E^1 = E + 1/2mv^2 + O(V^3)$.

If M emits two photons of equal energy ($\Delta E/2$) in frame F, with one moving left and the other right, then by conservation of momentum, M remains at rest and then by conservation of energy, the remaining energy in the body is $E-\Delta E$, and the new mass is $M-\Delta M$.

If in frame $F^{\wedge}v$, by $+16$ the rightward moving photon has energy $(1-V/C+V^2/2C^2+O(V^3))\Delta E/2$ $(20+)$ and then the leftward moving photon has energy $(1+V/C+V^2/2C^2+O(V^3))\Delta E/2(-20)$, then the body must have energy $(E-\Delta E)+1/2(M\Delta M)$ $V^2+O(V^3)$

If after adding everything together and comparing coefficients we find that the E in frame F after the emission is equal to the E1 in frame Fv before emission, then $E=MC^2$

Einstein's Theory is considered inspired by many. While math is about "more than one," or separation, many believe it ultimately leads back to the truth of One. Others consider it high art as well. The quotation above is essentially a breakdown or short form of the mathematical theory behind Einstein's mass/energy equivalence, with a lot of the explanation and some of the math left out as a matter of expediency. The full process can be readily accessed on the internet if you would like to pursue it further. It's presented here so that you can appreciate the complexity of the thinking involved and the inaccessibility of the math to the average person, yet how simple the conclusion is.

On the other panel was the following:

If $E = MC^2$, then $M = E/C^2$.

If all matter has mass, then all matter has energy.

If all matter takes up space, and space and time are relative, then all matter takes up time.

If all matter is simply energy occupying space and time, then the universe as we perceive it is an illusion.

Let's repeat the conclusion: "...the universe as we perceive it is an illusion."

Mathematics is a wonderful tool and has led to dramatic insights into the physical world that we have created and continue to create. It's a fascinating language to those who learn it, apply it, and appreciate it. To others, it's complicated and mind-numbingly boring because it's so hard to understand.

Conclusion

Both the quantum field/wave and the Higgs boson are at the limits of science and are evidence of an infinite, uncuttable part of existence similar to our definition of All-That-Is. Infinity is one of the attributes of All-That-Is, Heaven 2.0.

SECTION FOUR
CREATING FAITH AND TRUST

CHAPTER 15
NIRVANA, FAITH, AND TRUST

One of the most convincing arguments for the existence of Heaven is also perhaps the subtlest. Throughout history, people have noticed that people need other people, not only for procreation but also when problems arise, such as injury, illness, or the frailties of old age. There is the need for feeling good and the avoidance of pain. The desire to feel really good is there, too, if that is possible. Part of feeling good is building a workable, understandable, and trustworthy belief system that serves as a guide to navigating life.

The Search for Nirvana

When Heaven 2.0 is described, we're talking about unattenuated Love and Joy. Some spend lifetimes working up to it. The Catholics call it the "beatific vision," the "ultimate direct self-communion of God to the individual person." The Buddhists call it "nirvana," the "transcendent state in which there is neither suffering, desire, nor sense of self," a state of perfect happiness, an ideal or idyllic plane. Islam and Hinduism talk about Heaven as a place of pleasure as well, though the details differ. This is what we all remember at some level and often aspire to find again.

A whole lot of human behavior can be better understood as the seeking of pleasure or "fun." In Heaven, pleasure is undiffused, full strength, yet all of us reading this book chose a body knowing things would be different here. The world we have created doesn't allow much pleasure and what is available is diminished and doesn't last very long. We seek happiness in food, sex, relationships, money, competition and work among other ways. There are almost always unintended consequences, such as getting fat, having babies, fear of losing one's money, working too hard, addiction and death.

The human experience always seems to be a dichotomy, a split mind experience. The good times don't last, leading to mixed feelings. Birth always leads to death. The special people we love often get sick, have troubles, leave us or die; we miss them terribly. The pleasure of their company goes with them. The people we don't care for seem to have it in for us, probably because we blame our troubles on them. We vacillate between being awake and being asleep, day and night, good times and bad. Sometimes we wish to get rid of the bad times, other times we miss the excitement. There is the old saying, "And this, too, shall pass away."

Many seek a more perfect world and work to create it, yet have a hard time tolerating the other people who just don't get it. We seem to be able to tolerate a little pain and suffering if we know that there will also be occasional periods of happiness. We really like our body and want to keep it, along with the identity it provides. If there is a Heaven, we want to keep our body. After all, we define ourselves as the story of our body. We forget completely about perfect Love, Peace, and Joy most of the time because we have settled for just a little and it is enough.

Real Love, Peace, and Joy can't be found in a body, which was ultimately made as an experience of separation from the perfection of Heaven. We talked about the blocks to the remembrance of Heaven, and there are many thousands of schemes and ideas to keep us from opting out of physicality. We can deny, ignore, and fear all we want, but deep down the desire for Heaven never completely goes away! It's this deep desire that is real evidence of Heaven. We couldn't want it if we couldn't remember it or if it didn't exist.

Here is where the process of "undoing" starts. First of all, one must want Heaven 2.0 more than the physical universe, more than the bodies that go with it. No ifs, ands, or buts. You have to believe. You have to trust that you will be helped on your journey. You have to develop faith and trust. Permanent nirvana depends on it and there are many on the path to undoing the blocks and remembering our Oneness.

You Already Have Faith

All of us already have faith in some form. It's part of life. It can be pretty basic, such as faith that the sun will rise in the morning or that your parents love you. This faith helps us get up in the morning and guides our behavior throughout life, whatever it is. In a way, faith is the sum of what we believe and have experienced, which we rely on to negotiate our life. Faith is trust or confidence that something will be there when you get there, even though you can't see it from where you are. There's also the faith in belief systems, be they political, monetary, or religious. This ability to believe in other people is important to get through life efficiently. Every day would be a brand-new day if we had no faith or trust in anything, ever. Sadly, there are people for whom this is true, through disease or disorder.

No matter what one thinks about Heaven, Love, or Life, one must have a sense of faith in It in order to remember and overcome the blocks we have put there. It seems the closer we get to enlightenment, the more distractions there are to keep us from staying on the path. Many liken the world to the story about the swamp and alligators: when you are surrounded by alligators, it's hard to remember that your original goal was to drain the swamp; and the alligators have babies. Often problems demand immediate resolution, forcing us to look for answers to life problems rather than undoing the blocks to the remembrance of Heaven.

There are two competing belief systems, and they are mutually exclusive. Reality is either dual or nondual. You can see either the physical world and not Heaven, or you can see Heaven 2.0 and not the physical world. There really isn't a middle place where one can see both at the same time. This is essentially the role that faith plays: deciding which beliefs to hold until we can see the one we want. A "faithless" person usually goes the way the winds of Ego blow, never ending up on the road to Heaven 2.0 for very long. The dualistic physical world demands constant attention in order to remain alive, while faith in Oneness is required to see Heaven 2.0 because the physical illusion isn't Real.

Many of our beliefs and faith have come to us from other people, such as our parents, teachers, and religious people, starting from birth. We are no longer conscious of or even aware of most of these beliefs, yet they guide or control our decisions in life. The odds are overwhelming that the beliefs we hold subconsciously conflict with each other, causing even more consternation. Yet on any journey through life, it helps to know where we are going and how we are going to get there.

> If you don't know where you're going, you'll end up someplace else.
>
> –Yogi Berra

Faith in Dualism

The world is filled with people who will mock those who believe in Oneness and accuse them of childishness and insubstantial feelings. The dualists see no use for Oneness in the physical world unless it can be turned into a method of control over others in a world of scarcity and survival. It's seen as weakness. It's tough to believe in Oneness in the physical world, especially when it draws opposition.

It is almost impossible to get everyone believing the same thing for very long and the imperatives of the human body and the five senses usually prevail. Sadly, faith in physical things or human organizations is usually doomed to disappointment because everything in the physical realm changes and it isn't always for the better. Faith in money, government, religions, and/or technology usually fails when the human beings in charge fail to live up to their promises. Utopian and socialistic schemes seldom work for very long due to the changeable nature of the world, for they are based on dualism, specialness, and the need to be right.

The history of faith-based organizations rooted in physical reality is dismal and a real problem for someone who finally remembers Oneness and seeks the way to realize it. Part of the problem is that flesh-and-blood organizations depend on people's loyalty and contributions for their long-term survival. Their purpose is valuable, to keep alive the idea and memory that our Source is Heaven and help us practice love in all of our relationships. However, faith in a religion isn't necessarily faith in Heaven. One is trust in an earthly organization, the other faith in Reality. While religions got their start in trying to help us to change our focus from the physical world to Heaven and real Oneness, they aren't immune to the problems of an insane world.

Unfortunately, when founders of religions die, their dynamic teachings usually become petrified, be it stone tablets or holy books. Sometimes the ideas are interpreted in ways that are not necessarily what the founder meant. It's not always a bad thing: writing down and codifying dogma makes it easier to pass on the wisdom to people in the future. These teachings are usually a set of beliefs, activities, and behaviors, often external in nature and tailored for an historical group of people. Over centuries, things change and if the dynamics don't adjust, there are problems.

For many, religion is about obeying the rules and agreeing with what is taught, nor unlike paying insurance to avoid the possibility of going to Hell when they die. Sincere faith is an individual and internal matter; not everybody understands it. Real faith is a journey to remembering our Loving Source, our oneness with Oneness. The original teachings are meant to get us started – the rest is up to us.

When church people misuse money, sexually abuse children, or take advantage of church members in any way, it often destroys the faith of those involved. If a priest, pastor, or other religious teacher doesn't have sufficient faith by which to live their own life, how can they justify that faith to others? When otherwise peaceful religions teach that it's OK to kill people who don't believe in their faith, this results in a conflict between the teaching and the instruction on how to live. All religions teach about love, joy, and peace in many ways. Abusive leadership leads many to abandon their church altogether and be justified in doing so. The very essence of the teaching on how to return to Love has been compromised. The loss of faith and trust can take time to heal.

Developing Faith: Choosing Where to Place Our Trust

What we should believe in is perhaps the most important set of questions we will ever answer for ourselves because it will determine the course of our lives both here in the physical world and perhaps especially afterward. Whether we wind up going in circles and keep riding the mandala of physical bodies or making progress toward Oneness and waking up to Reality is at stake in the choices we make.

Many of us have trouble with faith in Heaven, and for good reason. Those who don't believe in something greater than themselves, in an eternal, all-encompassing Love and Peace, aren't going to look for it, and thus they will miss all the clues. Even if they did find it, they would ignore it and then deny they saw or experienced anything. They would dismiss it as "crazy talk." That's why sometimes it takes a life-threatening catastrophe for people to reevaluate their lives and beliefs.

Sometimes we can't see Heaven because of the problems we have created in our illusory world. Faith in Heaven means changing our minds about the world. Everyone in a body chose to be here and has made the decision to experience a unique individual body in the physical life, deliberately ignoring Oneness's eternal peace and love. It's a deterrent to believing in Heaven. Faith can only return when we reevaluate the physical world and overcome the addiction to the illusory body that we have. We have to decide that there must be a better way than life in a body, asking for remembrance of our real home, which we have never left, and starting to work on rolling back the obstacles to the remembrance of Heaven. We have to change our mind.

Another problem is that while some of the things we believe in are true, others don't work out. A big part of human history is the story of how our understanding of who we are has changed. We have to be willing to continue learning new things and change our minds about those things that have been shown to be false. This is to be expected since it's not possible to know everything. We live our lives based on our "faith" of the moment, altering it as we learn new things and have transforming experiences. This book is to help you remember your real home in Oneness so that you can find a way to reawaken into Love, Peace, and Joy.

Some consider faith a "gift," and many without it, seek it. Those who really like Earth and want to create Heaven here are likely to be disappointed. Since Earth is an illusion, creating another version of Heaven would be just that, – another illusion! It's best to go for the Real thing, Heaven 2.0. After all, you are already there and it works great! The thing is, to acquire faith means releasing our attachments to physical things and desires. Again, faith is really a choice, not so much a gift to add to one's collection.

Faith Is Hard Work

Those who have faith in Heaven must work to develop and maintain that faith. For many, faith is an individual thing, not always shared with others. Since it's individual, you might not notice faith on the outside, but many see that the person of faith acts with integrity and consistency within the beliefs they have acquired. The belief in the afterlife motivates people to learn as much about it as they can and to treat other people with care and consideration. Faith in Oneness predisposes a person to see and experience other evidences of Heaven, things that a nonbeliever would dismiss as meaningless or useless. Faith must be cultivated and adjusted as new insights and inspiration become commonplace in your life.

Faith is not static but rather is dynamic. When one expresses faith in something, time and the belief in separateness will challenge that faith periodically. Some experiences oppose faith in the unseen, others reinforce it. Most people feel their faith is guided by the thing they have faith in and learn to ignore the things that aren't helpful. Discerning what to ignore and what to heartily embrace is a basic challenge of living, and this is certainly true of faith. Now, if one can gain some understanding, it increases one's faith and makes it stronger. One must start with a little faith and act on it. You do have a choice of what to have faith in – and what not to trust. The material in this text is meant to help one strengthen their faith, not supplant it.

Exercising Faith Leads to Understanding

Faith is something to guide us through life. The beliefs of our faith can be likened to a smart phone with GPS, as faith opens our minds to inspiration and inner guidance. If you liken life on the physical plane here to a journey, we need guidance to get where we are going. The GPS shows you where you are and can often give you a choice of routes as to how you can get where you need to be. Some maps, some GPS's are better than others, and you soon learn whether or not you can trust yours by your experiences with it. When you get a good one, you stick with it.

Likewise, when you start finding that your inner guidance works and helps you get where you are going each day and helps you understand what is happening to you, this gives you some perspective on your perceptions. Many find that at first there is interference from the loud, interrupting Ego voice for separateness and its insistence on judgments of all kinds. One must learn to listen for the subtler voice for Heaven until it becomes second nature. As with any cell phone, sometimes you are out of range for a short time. This is where your faith is critical and can help you through "dark nights of the soul." Sometimes it's these black times that motivate people to look for a better way. Remember that most people, when totally desperate, start praying. If they dodge the bullet and are saved from certain disaster, many people say something like, "Thank God!"

In any case, the full development of faith is the very best proof of Heaven: you just *know* that Heaven exists. The fact that faith exists at all is an indication that we have a built-in connection to Life, even if we don't always use it or acknowledge it. When we explore our faith and move to understanding, that is the best proof of Heaven there is. It's the goal of all other proofs in this or any other book on Heaven.

The importance of an awareness of the things we believe in and have faith in can't be overestimated, as they tend to guide our actions and our choices. If you aren't sure what you believe in or have faith in, journaling is a good way to become aware. It's a start that can lead you to make changes that will help you make better choices, choices that are more in line with who you really are and where you want to go. This desire to understand and improve is another part of the faith process. Too many fall prey to "calcification of the attitudes." You are never too old to change your mind.

Don't wait until your life is almost over or you are on your deathbed to change your beliefs. It's often too little too late, with many unseen obstacles still in place. On the other hand, it's never too late, as life will present chances for growth, no matter what they are called here.

Most of us look for an "easy death." Here are some of the last words of people who were dying and could see through the "open door" to what lay before them:

> Jesus of Nazareth: "Father, into Your hands I commend myself. It is finished."

> Martin Luther King: "Be sure to play "Blessed Lord" tonight, play it real pretty."

> Pope Alexander VI: "OK, OK, I'll come. Just give it a moment."

> Thomas Edison: "It's very beautiful over there."

> Mata Hari: "Everything is an illusion."

> Emmanuel Kant: "It is good."

> Timothy Leary: "Beautiful!"

> Gustav Mahler: "Mozart! Mozart!"

> Wolfgang Amadeus Mozart: "The taste of death is upon my lips. I feel something that is not of this earth."

Steve Jobs: "Oh, wow. Oh, wow. Oh, wow."

These famous people's last words point to anything but nonexistence. It's when faith is truly justified.

> Angels are "ideas" of Heaven that hover near and all about us. We do not walk alone. We cannot be alone. The Love of Heaven surrounds us with these angels and we are never comfortless. [A reworded quote from ACIM Workbook Epilogue]

In the next chapter, let's look a little closer at what Heaven 2.0 looks like, a kind of overview that can only be shared as a myth. It's symbolic and metaphorical, but can trigger memories of your own!

CHAPTER 16
A MYTH AS EVIDENCE

A story, a creation myth is entered here as evidence of Heaven because it's helpful to understanding, so that we might believe again. When we believe, faith, trust, and wisdom follow.

Storytelling: Seeking Identity

One of the core ways we think of ourselves as separate is that we have a story of personal experiences to tell. There are no "stories," per se, in Heaven 2.0 since Heaven just "is." But here, there are beginnings and endings. There is danger, fighting and the overcoming of evil and misfortune. Plans go astray. Stories are a part of who we think we are and they give us clues as to how and why mankind wound up in the physical world. We are drawn to other people's stories, no matter how they are told.

Whenever you ask someone who they are, you get a story, often beginning with, "I was born..." followed by the events of their life. For many, it's the excitement of the chase that is the lure of storytelling, the curiosity of how things turn out. Our favorites often involve a "happy ending," or the overcoming of adversity.

Stories are metaphors in that we can relate to the fictional characters because they are just like us. From the point of view of Heaven, the story is just an illusion, an entertainment and not real. While listening to the story in our minds or on the movie screen, we pretend that it's real, ignoring that it's just a movie. We know the video isn't real: it's essentially dots of light on a screen with a sound track to make it appear real. There are no real flesh-and-blood persons actually on the movie screen. Still, we often value those fictional characters and consider them more real than a lot of people we have never met.

Many of us are addicted to stories and it's hard to say if they are just a way to pass the time, are a distraction from our real work or if they can be a way of passing on ideas and beliefs as to who we are, why we are here, and how we should live. It depends on the stories that we choose.

Stories are hard to avoid, from the gossip of neighbors and family members to the stories in books, videos, radio shows, podcasts, church sermons, advertising, and those told by coworkers and politicians. In any case, we are attracted to stories, the dilemmas, hardships, accidents, and evil that are often explored in them. Sometimes we can find answers and suggestions, sometimes not, but we all want to find out how "it works out in the end."

Stories and myths are an agreeable tool to share information that, for many, is the best and most convincing evidence of all. If the story makes sense and feels right, it can be a framework to get us to the direct experience where stories are no longer needed.

Myth: An Idea Takes on a Life of Its Own

Myths are often tailored to the audience, something that will give people an idea of what happened but is entertaining enough to keep their interest. There have been many in the past, yet Heaven 2.0 requires a different one, which we will get to shortly.

There are many "creation stories" extant that attempt to explain how we got to this physical world and why we appear to no longer be in Heaven, despite the fact that it's everywhere present. A recent Wikipedia article lists at least 50 such stories. Keep in mind that these stories are culture-specific and are regarded as conveying a deep truth to help people understand how the world started and why things are the way they are. They are a valuable tool for understanding in each culture.

Myths usually have a lot of symbolism. The words and the characters stand in for dimensions within Oneness that shifted creatively in ways that we can't really understand, though we might get a sense of what appeared to happen. Myths are not true in a historical sense, but can tell a symbolic story that is way beyond words to accurately describe. Much of what myths communicate is intuited directly.

A Course in Miracles contains an excellent discussion of what appeared to happen. Our myth here is partly based on that detailed symbolic story of what might have happened for this world to appear. *ACIM* starts the myth this way:

Into eternity, where all is one, there crept a tiny, mad idea, at which the Son of God remembered not to laugh. In his forgetting [to laugh] did the thought become a serious idea, and possible of both accomplishment and real effects.

This tiny, mad idea was essentially wondering if it would be possible to separate from the Whole. Now just what the phrase "Son of God" refers to is indefinite, because "Son of God" is a metaphor for an aspect of the creative part of Oneness. The Eternal I AM is unflawed, yet the Son of God is referred to as "an extension" of the Whole, but in a way that is totally nonphysical and not separate or different from Oneness in any way. Gary Renard found the words in his seminal book *The Disappearance of the Universe*:

What God [Oneness] creates in its extension of Itself is called Christ [in *ACIM*]. But Christ is not in any way separate or different from God. It is exactly the same. Christ is not part of God, it is an extension of the whole. Real Love must be shared, and the perfect Love that is shared in God's universe is beyond all human comprehension. Humans appear to be part of the whole, but Christ is all of it. The only possible distinction between Christ and God— if a distinction is possible—would be that God created Christ; He is the Author. Christ did not create God or Itself. Because of their perfect oneness, this doesn't really matter in Heaven.

> God has created Christ to be exactly like God,
> and to share His Eternal Love and joy in a state
> of unencumbered, boundless and unimaginable
> ecstasy. (p. 124)

A Myth

Within Oneness, in the swirling of Love and Ideas within the "Son of God, the Christ," a "tiny, mad idea" surfaced and was examined by the infinite Power of Heaven. Impossible ideas are generally the source of humor in Divine Mind, but with this one, laughter was not immediate. The idea? Could an idea separate itself from Oneness, could it experience itself as its own source? What does it feel like to be God? Oneness responded to the idea immediately, and it ceased to be a concern. Source allowed the idea of separation to be experienced within the all-encompassing Love and Power of All-That-Is. Knowing that nothing harmful could come of this idea, Oneness provided a way to experience the alluring idea of separation. The idea of individuality was fully explored in all its creative glory, but all resultant false ideas disappeared, as is always the case.

The separation was experienced "within a bubble," surrounded by Love, Power, Peace, and Joy. The idea was allowed to explode, a big bang that created an infinite number of ideas, and all possibilities were explored. Many of the resultant ideas, remembering their Source, didn't continue and returned, leaving the bubble of apparent separation because the Love

194

and Power of Heaven is home. Since all ideas have free will, the gift of their Source, others appeared to make different choices, all illusory experiences and incapable of changing Reality. All possible variations were explored.

A group of ideas consolidated into what is called Ego, a sense of self that thinks it's truly separated from Heaven. It realized that if it wanted to survive separately, it had to work to make the illusion real. If it could get other separated souls to forget Heaven, things could go on indefinitely. Failure would mean losing individuality and returning to Oneness. Ego was necessary for Source to allow the idea to be experienced.

Ego sprang into creative fury, a "bang" that involved the creation of the physical world, "the image and likeness of Heaven" so that souls could enjoy their newly found selves and not be just part of Oneness. Ego extended itself over and over and over again, infinitely, just as Oneness had, expanding the appearance of separation. The world we see is the result of this creative imaginary adventure. It appeared to be wonderful, beautiful, the most creative idea ever. The separation from Heaven appeared to be complete, yet the reality is that it is still an illusion, a mirror image, still in the bubble of forgetfulness. Ego focused on separation and completely and conveniently forgot that this whole experience was within Oneness.

Ego was full of itself and believed it was now its own source and that to continue to "exist," it must deal with the former Oneness, which it believes is a) no longer whole and b) is separate from Ego. At some point the idea of fear gripped Ego, for it began to realize it had injured or damaged Oneness, and that whatever was left of Oneness might not like it and might even try to punish Ego for what it had "done." That is what Ego would do if it were Oneness. It didn't realize that it was just one idea in an infinity of ideas and that there was no harm done of any kind. Nothing had really happened to change Oneness.

The fear of retribution festered and led to another idea because there was nowhere to hide. After all, the idea was still within the Whole. This fear of punishment was caused by a sense of guilt, of having done something wrong, something unforgivable, yet its very existence depended upon keeping the charade going. Ego didn't realize a separation never really happened. No real separation, no guilt, no punishment. Oneness is only Love.

Ego, in its fear of revenge and attack, acted against Oneness by dreaming up an infinite universe and "living" creatures in which to hide. Not just human bodies, but also all forms of life. These bodies are clusters of cells, molecules, and atomic structures that hide the mind in order to shelter it from being found and punished by Oneness. The goal was to create another heaven away from Heaven, to be its own creative source. All possible forms of individualization were explored within time and space for maximum differentiation and camouflage of the "Christ." Ego was happy, seeing the physical world as a place to hide "little pieces" of itself in such a way that the whole of Ego could never be found, blamed, and punished. Oneness was at once denied, forgotten, and ignored, mostly.

The bodies were fun and allowed the souls (individuated, separated little egos) to learn about something even Oneness couldn't provide—the knowledge of good and evil, life and death, health and sickness, light and darkness: duality.

One of Ego's most creative ideas was to project the fear and guilt they were all feeling for the apparent injury to Oneness onto other "individuals." This is the ultimate "blame game" where everybody blames everybody else. To keep life fun, they projected Love onto those they liked. To keep Ego alive and rid themselves of fear and guilt, they would project their negative feelings onto chosen others, who would become enemies. Therefore, specialness came into apparent being, reinforcing the "us vs. them" feeling that makes the whole scheme appear to be real. It's at the core of the concept "perception creates reality." Trouble is, few individuals really liked it when fear and guilt was projected onto them, but they reciprocated by returning the favor. The result was everyone has a split mind, part special good, part special bad, all sharing the guilt and far of Ego.

The creation of the physical universe and bodies is Ego's crowning glory as a self-perpetuating system of appearances: beginnings and endings, not eternity; not enough of everything vs. no worries; life is dangerous at times instead of Loving and Peaceful; and hatred, murder, attacks of all kinds keep the "individual" busy and occupied with the maintenance and survival of this world. Ego is always aware that the apparently "shattered" "Son of God" could remember Oneness if it wanted to, a remembrance that would bring the end of the entire thought system.

The Undoing and Correction of the Separation Idea

Heaven, in its Beauty, Splendor, Love, and Power, respected the free will of this insane idea and allowed it to be experienced. Each apparently infinitely replicated mind gradually realized that its "mirror world" was nothing compared to the one they all had tried to forget. Oneness gently allowed all ideas to awaken from their "drunken nightmare" in their "own time," in a way that no harm was done. Love allowed the idea of separateness to be expressed, honoring the free will that is an aspect of All-That-Is. In this allowing was the correction included, so that after the idea had been experienced, explored and found wanting, the creative love and beauty involved was preserved and illusions disappeared. In this way, Love was extended and all is well in Eternity, as it always has been and always will be. All crazy, impossible ideas are corrected, even as Love is grateful and appreciative of all creative aspects of Oneness.

From the "point of view" of Heaven, this physical world never really was. It appeared to last only an instant. From our point of view within time and space, we aren't quite ready to remember and return, but we will.

ACIM editor Ken Wapnick likened the idea to a roll of carpet. It came from Oneness, rolled out to its extreme, then rolled back up, disappearing into what you might call the memory of Oneness. It's impossible to really understand the dynamics of how it works until we ourselves remember and re-experience our oneness at the "End of Time."

> Life's but a walking shadow, a poor player
> That struts and frets his hour upon the stage
> And then is heard no more. It is a tale
> Told by an idiot, full of sound and fury,
> Signifying nothing.
> —William Shakespeare, *Macbeth*, act 5

As the author of *A Course in Miracles* famously wrote, mentioned earlier:

> Nothing real [Heaven 2.0) can be threatened.
> Nothing unreal [illusion] exists.

SECTION FIVE
HEAVENLY FAQ'S

CHAPTER 17
FAQ'S ABOUT HEAVEN

Objections to Heaven – Note Well

Nearly all objections to Heaven 2.0 revolve around the belief that we are separate bodies, that we are bodies, and that these bodies are the only life worth living. We want to keep it in as good condition as possible, stay in it as long as possible and we believe that when the body of a loved one ceases to work, we have lost that loved one forever.

Our premise is that the purpose of the physical world is to experience separation, learn about good and bad, life and death. The illusion of separation is a learning dream and cannot become permanent. It's hard to talk about Heaven 2.0 because the only reference we have is the physical and words that are made to communicate and reinforce a physical mindset. The perceptions of evil and separation aren't part of Heaven 2.0 at all. Heaven 1.0 is still about separation, punishment, and currying favor with a judgmental Deity.

Many hope that we as individuals will be reunited with the ones we loved while alive. If we retain separateness and individuality, that is not Oneness. It is not Heaven 2.0. Those who decline the invitation to Oneness in order to remain separate do just that, remain separate. What happens next is no more or less predictable than what happens on earth.

If you do not believe in any form of life beyond the physical, your objection cannot be addressed here, other than to note that you really need to examine your ideas about reality. If the physical is all there is, you really are asleep, having denied and forgotten your Source. Good luck finding a systematic understanding of who you are and your purpose or goal in life.

We will differentiate between Heaven 1.0 and 2.0 in our answers to frequently asked questions. Heaven 1.0 was created by Ego as a substitute Heaven and chosen by us when we chose separation. For some, Heaven 1.0 is "good enough" and means that they can retain individuality and separation from Oneness. It's just that Heaven 1.0 is not permanent and definitely not perfect. When we remember Heaven 2.0, we will need to release some preconceived ideas.

What is Heaven 1.0?

Heaven 1.0 cannot be precisely defined for a number of reasons. The most important of all is that it depends entirely on one's belief system and there appear to be billions of us, "all different and unique," or so we think. Just as we believe we are separate and unique from each other, the experience one has after death varies nearly as dramatically. The main feature of Heaven 1.0 is that separateness is maintained and includes our physical, possibly "glorified" body. This version of Heaven considers it to be all about personal pleasure and no physical or emotional pain. It is about "sitting at the right hand of the Father and giving Him glory." It gets kind of vague because it isn't an accurate remembrance of Reality. If Heaven 1.0 is all about the love of our body and God, then perhaps reincarnating into another body is allowed, after getting bored in Heaven 1.0. We get what we expect.

The love of bodies must be released before Heaven 2.0 can be embraced. The connection we feel for others in other bodies "still alive" or "lost" in the afterlife complicates and delays this discussion.

If we expect to see Jesus, Mohammad, Buddha, nothing, a saint or the Virgin Mary, we are most likely to be welcomed by an illusion that makes sense to us. We may have a separate "spirit body" and hope our loved ones still have their spirit bodies by which to recognize them. We think we get to keep it, no matter what else we experience, no matter how fantastic or mundane. Often our main focus in getting to Heaven is to be reunited with loved ones who have passed on. How else would we recognize them if they didn't have bodies of some sort? Pure Heaven 1.0.

Where is Heaven?

No one knows where Heaven 1.0 is. It's often referred to as up or in the sky due to metaphorical writings. Location is a function of time and space. Heaven 2.0 exists forever *outside* of time and space. Truly, time and space don't permanently exist and are a mere blip in eternity. For this reason, you could say Heaven is everywhere or even no-where. In eternity, the word "where" literally has no meaning.

How big is Heaven?

Size is relevant only in time and space. Size is a comparison of at least two things. St. John, in the book of Revelation listed measurements for Heaven (1.0), but in reality, he was relating a dream and did not personally make the measurements. Some people get put off trying to figure out how many people will "fit" into the Heaven they imagine, but it is totally beyond time and space. There is really nothing physical to compare it to and the descriptions are only given to help one imagine it at a specific time in one's development. Once we realize that there isn't anything else, we realize size is meaningless.

Do we have free will?

Yes, we are endowed with free will, but not quite like you might imagine. Heaven 2.0 didn't create individuals: there is only Oneness. Therefore, our free will is the same as that of Oneness, of which we are eternally a part.

First of all, we are exercising and exploring free will right now. The idea of separation, of trying to be our own source, is further evidence. Will is free, but we are not free to change Oneness, or Reality. The fact that we can't fully see, find, or experience Heaven 1.0 is a testament to the fact that we have chosen against Heaven 2.0, our Source. It is and continues to be our choice as long as we think we are a body of any kind. We have even put blocks to prevent ourselves from changing our minds easily, though we can do it if we want to. The only thing we are not free to do is to literally separate from our

Source. This temporary illusion of separate physicality is the best we can do.

The dictionary says free will is "the power to act without the constraint of necessity or fate, the ability to act at one's discretion." The only "constraint" on our free will is Reality. The idea that we can separate would mean changing Reality, the eternal, changeless All-That-Is. Free will within Oneness defies adequate description, but one could say that as long as our will is the same as Heaven's will, there are no limits. If our will isn't the same as Heaven's, then it is in error. It's doubtful that words will adequately satisfy on this subject. So, the answer is yes, we do have the free will of Heaven, except we can't change or destroy Eternity or Oneness. It works best when we are One with Heaven and Heaven's will is Our Will, as there is only One of us. It is circular and holistic.

If one considers the massive number of choices made by a near infinite number of people and other life forms throughout time and space, you can see clearly that free will or the ability to make choices is pretty much unfettered. There is just that one exception and it was "handled."

Will we be free to sin in Heaven?

Sin is an immoral transgression against "someone else." In Heaven 2.0 there is nobody else. The aspect of the One that we are has always had free will to create as we were created: one with All Things. Words aren't needed in Heaven, and there is no concept of sin. It's a meaningless idea. Since this world and our bodies were created as an attack on Heaven

2.0, we have already tried it. This illusory world is the best we can do. However, the best we can do is also a) insane and meaningless, and b) not of any consequence because it's not permanent and its apparent existence is merely an illusion.

In Heaven 1.0, we still think in terms of a body and define ourselves as a body and in that sense, we are capable of the fear and anger we brought with us from our life dream. Those who cannot let go might congregate in a state that some might call Hell. Hell is the denial of Heaven and some may create an experience that resembles their worst fears, either individually or in groups. Everything outside Heaven 2.0 is the world of separation and is by definition sinful. It is no more real than the illusion of our bodily life. In Heaven 2.0, where All-Is-One, our mind is part of the eternal God-Mind, so there is really no one to sin against. Since Mind is eternal, nothing sinful can happen, nor is there any reason for "self-harm."

Won't we be bored in Heaven?

Boredom means feeling tired because of nothing to do or not being interested in one's current activity. This is basically an ego "trick" based purely on having a physical body in the physical world. In a state of Joy without end, there is no tiredness (all-powerful), there is no end of creative activity (Heaven is endless creativity) and there is no possibility of "not being interested" because of the infinite nature of the creativity.

Oh yes, there won't be anyone to *be* bored, either. All is One. This Oneness makes little sense and is scary only to those in a body but is no more a big deal than a drop of rainwater falling into the ocean. The "drop" might not be a separate "entity" any more, but when it's reunited with the immensity of Love, it's filled with the Joy of its Source and boredom disappears.

Ego, the idea of separation, wants us to believe that All-That-Is is boring and that there is nothing to do. Words, again, fail us here. Boredom is unReal. Ego must justify the idea of separation and paints Heaven as sameness. Sameness on earth is boring, so Ego spreads the rumor that Heaven is boring because Oneness destroys the variety and excitement of separation. Oneness never changes and is by definition boring, according to Ego.

If you think about it, attack, depression, ignorance, and chaos in our physical world are truly boring since they endlessly repeat, ruining our idea of separation as a truly viable alternative to Heaven. Since Heaven is perfect, anything different from it (Ego) must introduce imperfection to contrast to the Real Experience. Since true separation isn't possible, our insane idea of time and space will eventually lose its luster and be abandoned as a "bad idea." It will be laughed at. It's the physical world that's truly repetitive, monotonous, and boring. It should be discarded, a thought that doesn't make the grade, compared to the Power, Love, Life, Joy and Peace that is Heaven 2.0.

Why can't we remember Heaven?

We could remember it if we wished to––and undo the blocks we have placed to reinforce our forgetfulness. We wanted so badly to separate from Heaven that we deliberately dreamed up the physical world as a place where we can forget about it and not have to remember. We deny it through our attempt to create a place where Oneness is not, but all we have succeeded in doing is creating a hell (any place where Heaven is not). We keep ourselves busy with the minutiae of being born, dying, surviving, getting sick, literally hundreds of things that make us think our bodies and those of other people are real. Some even create hell in the after-life, thinking they will be there for eternity.

Those who want to reopen the memory of Heaven 2.0 can do so through quietness and meditation. We have to dial down the senses of the physical world. Then, one by one, we have to undo the blocks we have erected to prevent our remembering. The still small voice of Reality instructs us on what to do if we listen. We can never completely forget, because that would mean forgetting completely who we are. Like the parable of the prodigal son, we eventually follow the promptings to stop slopping around with the pigs of evil and hatred, and return to Love, where we can again have everything, Oneness.

Heaven 2.0 isn't worried about us. The dream of separation is just that, a dream that is no more real than a dream in the physical world. It only lasts a brief moment in eternity. The Love of Heaven is eternal and patient. Because we have free will, the remembering must be our decision, aligned with eternity. Without the alignment, memory is difficult; it was our decision to go against Reality that started our difficulty in the first place.

How will we know our loved ones in Heaven if we must give up our identities?

When we die, we find our loved ones by feel and sometimes by sight. This happens early on, but as we awaken into Oneness, there is no need for special relationships, as all blends into Love and Joy such as we never knew on Earth. We find that we really love everyone and they love us—we are one and together in the most intimate way possible. The intimacy of Oneness is infinitely more compelling than is possible in a body.

Giving up a unique identity for the perfect Beauty of Oneness is like giving up having your feet cemented into a sidewalk. Once you are free of a passing identity, you will find that all your loved ones are really a part of you, but now without flaws, impediments, or time issues to get in the way of the fullness of the expression of love. The phrase "give up" is a misnomer, as you give up nothing and gain everything. To further the metaphor, once you can fly anywhere, you no longer miss having your feet in cement in specific body!

Will we know everything in Heaven?

In a word, yes. In this sense, Heaven is knowledge and in the sense that All is One, the One knows everything because there is nothing outside of it. There is nothing that's not part of Heaven, including what we think of as us. So yes, "we" will know "everything." In the sense that we want to know how things are going on Earth, who won this or who did that—not so much. The experience of separation in the physical world is a nightmare and isn't really happening. Literally nothing is happening in time and space except any expressions of Love. Believe it or not, when we reunite with the Loving Embrace of Love in Heaven 2.0, you will no longer remember the illusion of separation; it never Really happened and is of no consequence! Everything of consequence is already yours.

Will we all be equal in Heaven?

"We" won't be equal because there is no one to compare ourselves to. There is only Oneness. Equality is only important when you have a body and something to compare to. There isn't anything to contrast to, thus I Am. There is only "One" of us in Heaven 2.0. It is only in some ideas of Heaven 1.0 that the idea of specialness remains, a cardinal clue that Oneness has not yet been achieved.

What will we possess in Heaven?

Since neither Heaven 1.0 or 2.0 is a physical place, no physical items are needed or possible. The same goes for clothes, sex, food, and all manner of physical activities. It is said some people "go through the motions" of eating or sex or wearing clothes, but it is only in Heaven 1.0, where we think we are still separate from each other. The activity of Heaven 2.0 so far surpasses that of this world, physicality is not even remembered, much less desired. Remember the definition of Heaven given earlier. You not only own the universe, you are the universe. If you have no body, no needs, no real wants, no body functions, there is no need for possessions of any kind. If you still want them, you are earth-bound and not really in Heaven at all. Some say in Heaven 1.0 if you want something, all you have to do is imagine it, not unlike how we imagined this shadow world.

Is Heaven serious or funny?

These two words, "serious" and "funny," are relevant only in the physical world. In Heaven 2.0 there is only Joy. Joy is serious in the sense that it's important, consequential, and even momentous. On the other hand, if funny is a joke, strange, or suspect, then not so much. Serious and funny are really relevant to physical life, but not to Oneness. Yes, Eternity is seriously happy and joyful, but even Heaven 1.0 isn't a somber place or a place where people or things are made fun of in a condemnatory sense. The word "enjoyable" is more appropriate in an infinitely loving and appreciative way. Again, Heaven 2.0 is the feeling of Joy!

Is Heaven a myth?

The Greek-derived word "mythos" refers to a set of beliefs or ideas that are codified and mandatory and often identified with the very heart of each culture. These ideas give people something to believe in and provide a plausible answer regarding many of life's perplexing questions. For many centuries, what we call religion was actually a government-enforced myth, complete with mandatory religious practices. The myths were often treated as facts and required certain behaviors. This is still true in most religions. In common usage, a myth refers to a story or legend regarding usually supernatural events or experiences.

The word myth also carries the connotation of misrepresenting facts, of being false, fictitious, imaginary, or exaggerated explanations of said experiences. Many consider Heaven a myth, especially Heaven 1.0. However, myths have never been intended to be statements of fact or to be considered historically accurate, despite the fact that some treat them as such.

Religion was, for many societies in the past, more something one did, not something one believed in or had to prove, according to Karen Armstrong. You either did it or did not do it. You belonged if you did the religious practices; you were in trouble if you did not. Meeting your religious obligations helped give you the idea and feeling that you were doing God's will, not unlike paying the rent or buying insurance.

When books were rare and most people were illiterate, myths were used as a teaching tool to tell people about a lost paradise from which humans had been ejected in the very beginning. If people lived right, they could perhaps regain this Heaven they once had been in.

In a nutshell, myths about heaven abound, but the Reality of Heaven 2.0 is not a myth.

Does Heaven exist?

Heaven 2.0 exists by definition: it is All-That-Is. When we assume It exists, we are also including the "parts" of it that we cannot perceive with the five senses. There is nothing that is not part of All-That-Is. Finding it is a choice in our mind, not a perception of our senses.

Those who believe Heaven 1.0 is a separate physical place somewhere in the Universe and is a place of reward for living up to the tenets of a specific religion have yet to find it. Perhaps it doesn't exist in physical terms.

When were we created? Is it the same as when "life" begins?

The One, of whom we are forever a part, is eternal. Therefore, we are eternal; we have always existed and will never cease to exist. Science has been able to deduce that energy can't be created or destroyed. If this is the case, beginnings and endings are all illusion. Within the illusion of "disunion" or separation, moral issues surrounding the beginnings and ending of our earthly life are just one of many ways Ego keeps the illusion going, preventing us from waking up to the reality of Heaven 2.0.

To answer the question in this context, we have always existed. What we tend to call body creation or when a lifetime begins is a function of Ego and has nothing to do with Heaven 2.0.

CHAPTER 18
FAQ'S ON WHAT HAPPENS AFTER DEATH

The FAQ's in this section are mostly relevant to Heaven 1.0, not the full experience of Heaven 2.0. There is no real death in the sense that we cease to be or cease to think, love, or feel. We really only lose the dream world or illusion of our physical body. Birth is like waking up into a "new" reality and death is much like falling asleep and waking up elsewhere. These events are common to our earthly dream. Physical birth ties us to a specific body illusion until we choose at some level to break that connection at death. We fear death only because we identify so completely with the body involved and have come to believe that what we did in the body permanently influences what comes next. It's not true.

The range of experience after death is far more varied than most people would expect, owing to the vast numbers of people who think they are unique. Since we choose to create/enter a body in the physical plane where God is not, we have a choice as to what to do after our dream of being a specific person is over. If we still prefer bodies to our eternal union with Heaven 2.0, the next step can vary in many ways.

There does appear to be a life review and an evaluation of goals met or not, done by the person that chose the life, not a "Judging God." There is no global judgment day, but there appears to be a meeting with loved ones for many at the end of their lifetime. This also is optional, depending on the desires of the person. Dr. Moody's research on Near Death Experiences is outlined in Chapter 9.

The most important factor is one's state of mind. When one dies in confusion, fear, guilt, or hatred, those feelings don't just stop. If one expected annihilation, then darkness may prevail for a while. If one expected a religious figure, then the semblance of that religious figure may appear. If the person expected Hell, their vision of Hell may also appear for a time or perhaps just blackness for a while. Many slingshot back into a new human body to be with other individual like-minded "souls," (really another part of Self). Others stay in an afterlife world and plan their next lifetime, not yet free of the idea that the body and the world are worth saving. Unless it is Unity with All-That-Is, it is all the illusion of separation in its almost infinite variety geared to keeping us from remembering our Source and Home.

Those who have been able to release ALL attachment to the physical and to other life forms do have the chance to become one with All-That-Is, Heaven 2.0. They no longer are attached in any way to separate existence and willingly remember full Oneness. We call them enlightened, saints, masters, or angels. In any case, Love welcomes love.

What is limbo, purgatory, reincarnation, or *intermediate* heaven?

There appears to be a complete separation of souls and everything else in our physical world. Even the idea of an all-encompassing Oneness seems impossible and wholly foreign.

It makes sense to some that remembering and fully embracing Oneness might need to be done gradually, not unlike waking up in the morning for many sleepy-heads, one eye at a time. For others, it is like peeling back layers of "distractions" that delay awakening and for other it is like climbing up a ladder from a pit of self-imposed darkness to the light above: one step at a time. Whether it involves reincarnation, a planning place/time, recuperation, or something else, it could be called an intermediate Heaven 1.0, still part of the illusion of separateness.

The definition of Hell is anywhere where God is not. Most people experience periods of time in the physical world that are truly nightmarish, miserable, depressing, and tormenting. Beauty and Love do shine through regularly, making their opposite scary. Most of us actually seem to like this fruit-salad mixture of good and bad, life and death, at least for now. We don't want it to end. For many of the reasons discussed earlier about the blocks to Heaven, few humans wake up immediately into Oneness at death. It can happen, but most drag their feet, so to speak.

People tend to get what they expect, and there are few things that apply to all, except that all roads lead to the same place, Oneness. The dream of separation explores all possibilities, all of which must be undone as directed by our Source. Perhaps this "intermediate period" is also a good one to remind us of the absolutely repetitive and often negative nature of this dream and to use it to make progress toward Oneness. This limbo, this purgatory, this school can remind us of the uselessness of not-Heaven. In any case, it is highly individual and, by all standards, illusory. It is not Oneness or Heaven 2.0.

Is there a judgment after death?

As noted earlier, the only judgment after death is our own self-judgment. It's based on our decision to enter a body in the physical plane and our determination of whether it was "successful" or not. The judgment is a very individual thing and isn't done by some overarching super being, anthropomorphic at best. Heaven isn't a person, and neither are we, despite appearances. Heaven is Love, Peace, and Joy; so are we. Any appearance to the contrary is an illusion and is false. We only think things happen in this world, but they are no more real than a nightmare. Because nothing really happens, there can be no judgment other than self-judgment.

This is not to say that some people haven't used the threat of God judging people and punishing them with eternal damnation as an argument to get people to act in certain ways, usually to the best interest of the person arguing. Within the illusion, it's very possible for people to judge themselves, but there is no external entity that judges or condemns us. From the perspective of Heaven 2.0, the illusion of our lifetimes never really happened. If they never really happened, then there is nothing to judge and we are innocent, as we have always been.

Is there music in Heaven?

Yes, there is music throughout the physical universe and Heaven, but not necessarily in physical "earthly" forms. Music is a form of Joy and Love, in ways literally not accurately describable. In Heaven, we will *be* the music in every way imaginable. Remember we have no physical ears in Heaven.

Do people in Heaven see us now?

A better wording of this question is, "Do people in Heaven have bodies to see us as bodies on Earth?" The answer is: our loved ones are always with us inside and as such are never far away. On the other hand, this world is temporary and nothing temporary exists in Heaven. In that sense, there is nothing to see. Do they love us? Yes, immeasurably. Are they concerned with our small issues or nightmares? Probably not. Even in Heaven 1.0, souls realize that lifetimes are voluntary and the worst that can happen is to die and come back to the "after-life." Worries belong in the physical world and the only people who might worry in the afterlife are those sometimes referred to as "earth-bound." These souls died, but refused to leave the physical space, confused about nearly everything.

Do angels exist?

Definitions are an earthly thing, but there are angels in the intermediate world, upon whom we can call on here. Whether they are ex-humans or have never been here is absolutely not important or real. Angels are one of the helps given us along the way, both in physical life and in the intermediate world, to help us remember our Home and to guide those ready to return to it. They are a help, never forcing anyone to do anything. They are truly "ideas" given us when we need them. They are a function of Oneness, not a physical or spiritual "form."

Angels can "intervene" in our earthly dream to help us remember that Heaven is real. But since we always have free will, we determine what we experience on Earth or in any other physical place. We can be any life form anywhere in the physical universe, no restrictions, because it doesn't truly exist in the first place. In any case, if we want help and ask for it, it's usually given, even if we don't like the form it's given in or the timing of it. There are many who feel that a loved one is around them, guiding them through life. This is just one of the ways help is given. In that sense, angels exist. One must always remember that Oneness is the Reality. The appearance of a separate entity, no matter how wonderful, is still an illusion.

In the sense that All-Is-One is Heaven 2.0, angels are not separate beings as we know them. But since we do believe in separateness (as evidenced by the bodies we have), yes, angels appear in a way that we can accept.

Can we store up treasure in Heaven?

The very thought of storing up treasure is a turnabout of reality, as are so many ideas in the physical life. Heaven *is* the treasure, *we* are the treasure. Nothing physical can be a real treasure as there are no physical needs in Heaven—not money, not good deeds, not anything concerning a body. So, the answer is no.

There are many human beings who would exhort others to give them money, property, or other goods or services in the physical world in order to "store up treasure in Heaven," but it doesn't work that way in Heaven 1 or 2.

In a very real way, in Heaven 2.0 one gains remembrance of Everyone, All-That-Is. That treasure is already there and cannot be added to or subtracted from.

Can we or should we try to re-create Heaven 1.0 on Earth?

The simple answer is "Why would you want to?" The real Heaven 2.0 already exists now and everywhere. The idea of separation and Ego's creation of a mirror world with individual bodies is the ultimate "Heaven on Earth." That's what this is, right here and now – a fake pretend Heaven. It doesn't work because it is the opposite of the Real Heaven 2.0.

The Real Heaven is perfect and our mirror illusion must be opposite and imperfect or one could not tell the difference; besides we asked to learn about good and evil, and life and death, among other things. The problem with creating "Heaven on Earth" is that it means keeping physical bodies and individual status, which aren't possible in Heaven 2.0, nor is it even desirable. Those who want to continue to try to "perfect" this world are trying to resolve the unresolvable: making separation permanent.

Getting everybody who appears to be in a separate body "on the same page" emotionally, politically, financially, or spiritually is a pipedream created by Ego to make sure that the Real Heaven 2.0 remains ignored and forgotten. The very individuality it fights for is the one thing that cannot happen; when the illusion disappears, so does Ego. As the embodiment of the idea of separation, it fights to keep us distracted and entertained as much as possible, keeping itself "alive."

To Ego, the idea of creating a Heaven on Earth is seductive, to say the least. A perfect society would mean that a huge number of individuals would have to agree on certain specific behaviors, that is, "unify" or become one cohesive group. It just can't happen here because this world was designed for disunity, not oneness. More than five billion individuals with free will live here; they all want to be individual and not like everybody else. Creating Heaven on Earth is merely a delaying tactic.

Let look a little closer, as this is a very popular dream. Many idealists have surfaced with ideas on how to create Utopia. Their argument is simple: since a physical Heaven can't be found, it's up to us to create one right here and now. Many books have been written on the subject. Examples include St. Thomas More's *Utopia* (1516), in which he talked of an ideal and imaginary island nation of the same name; Karl Marx's *Manifesto of the Communist Party* (1848) and *Capital* (1867); and *How to Achieve a Heaven on Earth* (2012), a collection of contemporary articles edited by John Wade II. These books have inspired many to try to create a perfect global society on physical Earth. All assume that life on Earth can be "perfected," though just what "perfect" means isn't always defined or agreed upon.

All attempts at building a physical "Heaven on Earth" have proved futile for two very good reasons.

The first is that Utopias almost always involve forcing some people to act the way the "enlightened leaders" want them to. Utopias only work if *everyone* buys into the "rules" and no one slacks off, doing their share. Utopian societies wind up having to force those who slack off to comply. People get tired, lazy, bored or whatever excuse justifies not working as hard.

Second, those who work the hardest eventually want to be rewarded proportionately to their efforts. They notice the slackers and are tired of working to support those who could do the work, but won't. Both groups wind up destroying the initial premise of everyone getting along for the common good. People are supposed to work as hard as they can, and the hardest workers make up for those who can't work. Many people are good at "gaming" whatever system is put into place. They are really good at coming up with excuses why they shouldn't have to do their share; after all, they are "special" or they are victims.

After a lot of "shouting," the answer for leaders is either dissolution of the community when it fails or totalitarianism, forcing people to do the "right thing," completely destroying the Love, Peace, and Joy that Utopia was supposed to bring.

There are no examples of utopias working long-term without one or the other result. Even the forcing of people to comply brings an end to what was once a shining aspiration and plan for a perfect "heaven on earth."

In a nutshell, there can be no lasting Heaven on Earth. It's just another attempt to make the illusion of detachment from Oneness real. There is no "justice" in Heaven because there are no transgressions, no one to transgress against. There are no needs, wants or victims, so there is no inequality. There is only Unity, only perfect Oneness, the real Utopia. Heaven 2.0 already exists for the remembering.

Will there be an end of the world that we have to worry about?

In a very real sense, the end of the world will be like waking up from a nightmare. This nightmare involves what life would be like without Heaven. We seem to be stuck in this world, a strange mix of beauty and ugliness, love and hatred, poverty and wealth, justice and unfairness, and depression and exhilaration.

The physical world, as we know it, is not eternal. Observations by astronomers indicate that worlds are being born and others are dying. There are estimates that the Earth's sun will last only about 1,000 billion more years, after which it will cool off and turn into a burnt-out, frittered space rock.

From the standpoint of Eternity, the physical world came and went in a flash. The nightmare-dream we are experiencing was corrected and disappeared. The many remembered they are One.

Another metaphor is that Heaven 2.0 is like a parent slowly helping a child wake up from a nightmare. The parent shows love and respect, allowing the child to wake up naturally, all the while comforting them and telling them that they are safe and sound in their own bed at home. The nightmare disappears and is forgotten in the joy of being home and realizing that nothing bad had happened. This parent-child metaphor helps many to understand a little bit about what is going on. The biblical story of the prodigal son is also an excellent metaphorical account of how the world ends, in the joy of returning home.

CHAPTER 19
FAQ'S ON HELL

Do Hell and the devil exist?

The simple answer is that Hell and the devil only exist if you choose to experience them by being born in a physical body. There is no such thing in Heaven 2.0. We have said that Hell is anyplace where Heaven does not appear to be and very few say they have found Heaven on Earth. Since everything on Earth is an illusion, Hell and the devil are illusions, the same as all the other illusions.

Most people believe that God created this world and us as individuals. If God created this world, then He is also responsible for the evil activities we find here. Heaven did not create this illusory world, we did. We have made a god of Ego, the idea of separation. We are a part of All-That-Is, true, but Heaven did not create separation––that is impossible. Our creation of this world as an attack on Heaven, for we wanted a place without Heaven, the definition of Hell. Evil is our choice and exists only in our minds.

The Genesis story tells of the choice to eat fruit from the tree of the "knowledge of good and evil." When the choice was made to experience separation, the world of good and evil was created. We wanted to explore the ramifications of an existence that seems to be filled with opposites; the opposite of Paradise is Hell. Heaven 2.0 allowed the illusion to be examined briefly and we are in the middle of that experience now.

For this reason, Hellish behavior is experienced by many in this illusion. The many victims of terror, torture, slavery, theft, rape, and abuse of all kinds describe their experience as horrendous. All people who have bodies suffer from something, including depression, sickness, catastrophic injuries, and/or emotional abuse. While we are in bodies, having forgotten these choices, we are angry at anyone who might suggest that we have any part in this, that it is essentially "our fault." Part of Hell is projecting our fear and guilt onto other people, guaranteeing that they will be angry at being attacked by our projections. When they fight back, it isn't our fault; it never is, if we can help it. The Reality is that it's all an illusion in the end, though it is an awful nightmare.

However, this isn't the traditional place of Hell, as many believe it isn't imposed until after death, depending on behavior in this lifetime. Still, the definition stands: when you aren't experiencing Heaven, you are experiencing Hell; it could be before, during, or after a physical lifetime. We created our very own Hell mixed in with love and beauty. It's like manure in our desert; its a good thing it's an illusion and only temporary.

Evil and its personification, the *devil*, exist only inside our minds and are only as real as the entire illusion of physicality is. The experience of evil feels real, but it's only a nightmare within a nightmare, a perception based upon activities of bodies. If you take the bodies away, evil and the devil go away, too. Evil is a misuse of the creativity that is ours as part of Heaven, but we can't create in Reality against our nature; we can't create not-Love. It's an illusion within an illusion.

We are slowly awakening to the realization that there is not only no real opposite of love, but it wouldn't be worth it if there were. A world without love really is Hell. A world with both love and hate is still a world with Hell in it. Any world with Hell in it is unacceptable for a permanent reality, even if it were possible. So, while we "believe" and "experience" Hell and demonic personalities, they are not permanent, and as such cease to exist when we take our attention away from the illusion.

Why does Heaven permit evil to exist?

This is a very common question, and it also deserves a bit more explanation. Assuming you have read the above question, you should conclude that evil doesn't exist in Heaven. Heaven 2.0 is Love and is permanent; evil is a temporary illusion, a blip that was corrected immediately. Evil cannot exist in Heaven; there is nobody to harm another. There are no others.

Our physical world is an illusion, a nightmare, and is not permanent. It never really happened. Heaven did permit the idea of separation to be explored in a dream, but does not "permit evil to exist in Reality." Since evil only appears to exist in the illusory world, and the illusion never really happened, evil never existed either.

Heaven affords Its creations free will, the ability to create as It does. There is one structural exception: ideas can't create against or change Source, of which they are an integral part. Evil is an idea that is part and parcel of separation. The idea of separation was allowed by Source to be "imagined" because of free will, knowing that it is incapable of actually happening. Real separation can't occur, but a highly realistic simulation was imagined and allowed as a teaching/learning tool. One of the primary lessons we are learning is that detachment from Heaven doesn't work and is awful. Separation causes fear: that is a given. Evil stems from that fear and is blamed for it. Often evil is somebody's idea of what is good for them; it just happens not to be good for another, especially if they are blamed for problems the "other" is having.

The existence of evil is our choice. When we no longer want it, we can wake up, which dissolves our illusion of separation. We will find that nothing really happened. Just as we go to the movies and see the Earth blown to smithereens, when we leave the theater, the Earth remains the same: nothing really happened. In the same vein, evil never really happens, either; it's all part of the illusion of disconnectedness. Heaven 2.0 understands this and extends love to us always.

Are people who have been bad going to Hell?

The simple answer is that no one is really "bad," but all of us have chosen to be born into this nightmare illusion to experience what it's like not to be part of Heaven. This world is by definition Hell, so in a sense we've all gone to Hell! That doesn't make us bad. In fact, if nothing Real happened, we are all still innocent.

If a person lives their life in confusion and doesn't express love, odds are they won't be a different personality when they pass on, which is to say they will remain in a hellish place. Those who focus completely and exclusively on being alive on Earth and in a body, are known in some circles as "earthbound." It's part of Ego's "self-defense" plan to prevent the inevitable, the dissolution of the illusion.

This won't go on forever, as all of us will eventually remember and awaken from the untenable ordeal we thought up. So, you could say we all went to Hell for a while, but then decided to go back home. We are the prodigal son. It will be like we never really left and can now really appreciate Life for what it is.

AFTERWORD

Heaven 2.0 doesn't need to be proven. It just *is*. What can't be proven is this imaginary physical world. Remember: the simplest way to disprove it is to remember that without a body or the five senses, nothing in the material world is perceptible. The problem is that without sensory input, there would be no physical evidence at all. Rene Descartes, the pioneering French philosopher and mathematician, whom we have talked about in chapters two and seven, is one who considered that possibility, saying,

> When I consider this carefully, I find not a single property which with certainty separates the waking state from the dream. How can you be certain that your whole life is not a dream?

The film series "The Matrix" has this idea at its core. In any case, it's a mistake to think of the material world as real, as limited as it is in time and space. Our physical body's perceptions are limited. Yes, Heaven is mental but that is Reality, the changeless Eternity. The physical world just appears to be permanent because that's how we wanted it to appear. It doesn't take much to demonstrate that the world is unstable, unpredictable, temporary, and sometimes "dangerous."

The idea of separation, the ego, fought to keep the "life" we gave it. We empowered this idea and after considering it, changed our minds. The good and beauty that separation created is part of All-That-Is. That which is false will cease to appear to be and in fact has never been. The problem is that we in bodies can't tell the difference. That must be left up to Heaven, in whom all trust ought to be placed. After all, there is nothing else! Let us focus on Love, Peace, Joy, Power, and Wisdom – and nothing else!

ABOUT THE AUTHOR

Raymond Kresha is a former Catholic seminarian, journalist, teacher, and counselor. This book started after his mother died while he was in the seminary at age 19 and intensified after a near plane crash nearly cost him his life. He has studied many writers and spiritual disciplines before settling on A Course in Miracles. Much of this book has been channeled over decades as a personal learning experience, then refined for presentation here with the help of the Holy Spirit. He and his wife appear to live in the Texas Hill Country.

Printed in the United States
By Bookmasters